MAY *the* OWL CALL AGAIN

A Return to Poet John Meade Haines, 1924-2011

RACHEL EPSTEIN

MAY *the* OWL CALL AGAIN

A Return to Poet John Meade Haines, 1924-2011

An intimate correspondence of words, writings, and letters
with reflections on life, death, and friendship

RACHEL EPSTEIN

Cirque Press

Copyright ©2024 Rachel Epstein

All rights reserved. No part of this publication may be reproduced, distributed or transmitted in any form or by any means, including photocopying, recording, or other electronic or mechanical methods, without the prior written permission of the publisher and author, except in the case of brief quotations embodied in critical reviews and certain other noncommercial uses permitted by copyright law.

Published by Cirque Press

Sandra Kleven — Michael Burwell
3157 Bettles Bay Loop
Anchorage, AK 99515

Print ISBN: 979-8-89145-590-0

May the Owl Call Again: A Return to Poet John Meade Haines, 1924-2011
9798891455900
Library of Congress Control Number: 2023913565

The hardcover edition is the sole format of the book.

cirquejournal@gmail.com | www.cirquejournal.com

Back Cover photo, "Tanana River Valley" by Ray Bonnell
Book Design by Emily Tallman | Poetica and Carly Egli
Book Cover Design by Emily Tallman | Poetica

Disclaimer: Rachel Epstein claims sole responsibility for the contents and views presented in *May the Owl Call Again: A Return to Poet John Meade Haines, 1924-2011.*

Credit: John Haines, "Night" and "The Glutton" from *The Owl in the Mask of the Dreamer: Collected Poems.* Copyright © 1996 by John Haines. Excerpts from "The Creative Spirit in Art and Literature," from *Fables and Distances: New and Selected Essays.* Copyright © 1996 by John Haines. Excerpt from "With an Axe and an Auger" from *The Stars, The Snow, The Fire: Twenty-Five Years in the Alaska Wilderness.* Copyright © 1989 by John Haines. All reprinted with the permission of The Permissions Company, LLC on behalf of Graywolf Press, graywolfpress.org

Credit: John Haines, "On the Street" and excerpts from "Wartime: A Late Memoir" from *Descent: Selected Essays, Reviews, and Letters.* Copyright © 2010 by John Haines. Reprinted with the permission of The Permissions Company, LLC on behalf of CavanKerry Press, Ltd., cavankerrypress.org

This book is for Michael Brian Mitchell and the people of Alaska who have found love and friendship in unexpected places.

*The land gave up its meaning slowly,
as the sun finds day by day
a deeper place in the mountain.*

from "Homestead"

There will be much to remember.

from "Harvest"

ACKNOWLEDGMENTS

The publishers of Cirque Press, Sandra Kleven and Michael Burwell, and I gratefully acknowledge Joy DeStefano, wife and representative of the estate of John Meade Haines, for her cooperation and permission to use all writings of John Haines contained in this work.

Kathleen W. Tarr, Julie Hollowell, Rebecca Goodrich, Kenneth L. Privratsky, and Lael Morgan (1948-2022) encouraged the publication of *May the Owl Call Again: A Return to Poet John Meade Haines, 1924-2011* and offered supportive and constructive comments over the years.

Sandy Kleven's "Free and Open to the Public--An Interview with Rachel Epstein," in *Cirque: A Literary Journal for Alaska and the Pacific Rim:* Vol. 10, No. 2, 2020, was the first time I shared my relationship with John Meade Haines to a public audience. That there are so many people interested in his life has made a world of difference to me given our often self-indulgent universe.

A large thank you goes out to Mike Burwell, Teri Carns, Gretchen Diemer, Leslie Fried, Gene Irvine, Mary Kancewick, Sandra Kleven, David McElroy, John McKay, Doug Pope, Karen Tschannen, Paul Winkel, and Tonja Woelber whose financial support has made the publication of this book possible.

Rachel Epstein

Something About Alaska….

The importance and influence of Alaska Native peoples, their presence, and contributions to the whole of Alaska cannot be overstated. As of 2023, there are 228 Alaska Native tribes that are officially recognized by the Federal government and the State of Alaska. The Fairbanks North Star Borough, where John Haines lived, is within the traditional homeland of the Lower Tanana Dene people and to many other Athabascan, Gwich'in, and Inuit peoples who live in the region.

Alaska gained statehood in 1959 and contains approximately 365,000,000 acres of land. When the Alaska Native Claims Settlement Act (ANCSA) passed in 1971, Alaska Native land title throughout Alaska was extinguished. In exchange for land ownership, thirteen for-profit Alaska Native regional corporations and over 200 Alaska village corporations were created.

To this day and over multiple generations, legal battles concerning Alaska Native rights, relationships to traditional lands and the subsistence lifestyle continue to be fought and defined.

CONTENTS

Introduction	1
Part I. Words, Writings, and Letters	7
Alaska Writer Laureates' Panel	9
Three Poems	23
"Dear Rachel," Letters 2009-2011	29
Part II. Life Between Poetry and Place	141
Discord and Dissonance, Ending Thoughts	143
Five Poems and an Essay	149
An Overview of Contrasts: John Haines' Life Between Poetry and Place	169
A Sun, Distant Within: Eleven Poems and an Essay	181
Part III. Appendix	215
Correspondence Timeline	217
Notes	220
Publications and Selected Recordings	223
Index of Writings	226
Publisher Acknowledgments	228

John Meade Haines, Anchorage, Alaska, 2009 (*Photo Credit: Lila Vogt*)

INTRODUCTION

Poet John Meade Haines died on March 2, 2011 in Fairbanks, Alaska. I have transcribed our correspondence during the last two years of his life and titled the compilation *May the Owl Call Again: A Return to Poet John Meade Haines, 1924-2011*. It integrates a collection of John Meade Haines' words, writings, and letters to offer an intimate look into the last years of his life.

    Nationally acclaimed, John Meade Haines is known as Alaska's greatest poet, one whose literary stature rises high above Robert Service and Jack London. People from all walks of life have tasted the sweetness of his literary canon and become enamored by the mastery of his expressions and storytelling. This poetry transcends generations, landscapes, and human constraints that dwell in history and language. John Meade Haines' personal attention to his writings, from within and without, brings deep joy and understanding to those willing to see beyond their own breath toward an awareness of the precious life we each inhabit. This type of poetry is not for people who depend upon labels. It is written and shared for anyone willing to open their world to a kind wildness that comforts and confronts day-to-day existence. It is written in appreciation. It is poetry beyond poetry. It is poetry in friendship.

"In the Forest Without Leaves" welcomes one to a place where untamed nature exists in an age of degeneration, where observation is transformed into memory.

IN THE FOREST WITHOUT LEAVES XI

How the sun came to the forest:

How the rain spoke
and the green branch flowered:

How the moss burned
and the wasp took flight,
how the sun in a halo of smoke
put an end to summer.

How the wind blew
and the leaves fell.

Death made a space in the forest
where snow would come,

and silence, and night.

Like found leaves gathered, here are remembrances from when we first met and the friendship that developed.

ॐ

It is 2009, I am waiting for John Haines to arrive at the Ted Stevens Anchorage International Airport. He is 84 years old, traveling from Fairbanks to participate in the Alaska Writer Laureates' panel. Escorted, in a wheelchair, he appears with a cane in his lap.

Once in the car, I learn about John's life outside of Alaska, where he lived, travelled, and taught. I share with him a short version of my family's history, my previous studies, and current life with Brian. Numerous topics surface in rotation. At some point, John mentions the political philosopher Rosa Luxemburg. The conversation becomes so intense that I miss the turnoff for the hotel and have to circle round.

At the Alaska Writer Laureates' panel, held on April 1, 2009 at the UAA Campus Bookstore, four Alaska laureates answered questions about their lives, connections to Alaska, and scholarly work. John addressed attending art school in the East, venturing to Alaska, his homestead, writing ambitions and literary influences. Students in the audience appeared fully engaged while captivated by John's stories.

John recounted how as a young man applying for work as a draftsman in Washington, DC, he noted his formal art education on the application. In a stern way, the supervisor had warned him, "Remember, we don't want any malcontents here." As if, in John's reflection, being an artist meant a life of existential gloom. Everyone laughed.

John recited the poem "Winter News" and an earlier poem "Untitled," written after his wife Peggy had left Richardson to return to New York City for good. The last line, "New vines will grow again next summer, but you will not come back" swept the room with a sad quiet.

Towards the end of his allotted time, in a more serious tone, John described the people he knew in "With an Axe and an Auger" and the marks left behind from people who worked the land. "They are useful ghosts, these old inhabitants with their handwork implements, their settled lives. They tell us something of what we have been, and if we live long enough and well enough, what each of us may become: one more sign of our residence on earth, alive by reason of remembered love."

This sentiment of remembered love is a theme that echoes throughout many of John's poems. What struck me was how John coupled the human imprint on landscape with the human impact on nature.

When we returned to the airport for the flight back to Fairbanks, an attendant at the ticket gate offered John a wheelchair. When she mentioned her father liked poetry, John immediately stopped to give her the CD *Winter Light, the Poetry of John Haines*. She was simply elated by his kind gesture. This type of gesture is how I remember John Haines.

After John's visit, we began to write cards and letters to each other on a regular basis. It was as if seeds from the past found ground to rest in. I was familiar with Classical Chinese poetry, delighted with prose poet Russell Edson, and impressed by the artists Hans Hofmann and Franz Kline. Moreover, I had studied 19th century European history 30 years earlier, which, unbeknownst to me, became somewhat significant in our correspondence. That John studied Chinese poets in translation, had approved of Russell Edson in a book review, had attended the Hans Hoffman School of Art alongside Franz Kline put us in familiar mindsets, even though we were generations apart. In one letter he included his essay "On the Street," a story about his art school days in New York, which is quite honest, observational, and personally revealing.

A few months later, in late June, John returned to Anchorage for the USA Artists gathering, which happened to coincide with his 85th birthday. Joining him was Fairbanks composer John Luther Adams, also a recipient of the prestigious fellowship. When I met them at the airport, both were in good spirits—referring to each other as Adam and Eve, JLA twirling around, acting silly—as we walked through the baggage area to the car.

Later that week, poet Tom Sexton (Alaska Poet Laureate, 1995-2000) and other literary folk celebrated John's birthday at a local East Indian restaurant. It was a rare occasion, having two formative Alaska poets together at the same dinner table in Anchorage. In no time, halfhearted poetic rote and fuzzy memories crisscrossed the table for everyone to hear.

After our initial meeting in April, John began to send me humorous cards with funny notations. He claimed we would see each other again, here on earth or in the next life. In the correspondence, John would offer literary reflections while responding candidly to my questions. Although very much in the present, his jovial nature could not cover up the dire situation he faced—aging, with little income, deteriorating health, and few people around who understood his eccentric behavior and dependence on care.

From cards and letters, we established a correspondence that may sound more or less than what it was. I found someone to converse with about things that, at one time, had been on my mind—questions left unresolved by overthinking or put aside due to the demands of daily life. And John found someone who respected what he thought and had a genuine concern for him.

Writing his final book, *Descent*, gave John the opportunity to focus on what he felt was important in life and what was important in his life. Published in 2010 by CavanKerry Press, it received a two-line blurb in the *Anchorage Daily News*. By compiling *May the Owl Call Again*, my hope is that more people will discover John Meade Haines and become intrigued by his life and literary accomplishments.

Sourced from a deep friendship, may these little bits and pieces of John Haines live on.

Rachel Epstein

PART I.

Words, Writings and Letters

ALASKA WRITER LAUREATES' PANEL

The first Poet Laureate of Alaska was appointed in 1963. The title changed to Alaska State Writer Laureate in 1996.

The Alaska Writer Laureates' Panel, held on April 1, 2009, included John Meade Haines (1969), Richard Dauenhauer (1981), Anne Hanley (2002), Nancy Lord (2008) and acting as moderator Kathleen Tarr. Questions directed to John Meade Haines from the panelists and audience, including Walter Parker who moved to Fairbanks, AK in 1946, are offered here. To capture John Meade Haines' voice and to better understand his early life, I suggest reading his responses, transcribed here, out loud.

Question to laureates: In what ways has Alaska influenced and informed your artistic journey? How has this landscape contributed to your creative vitality?

John Haines: I think I have said all that I can say about that. Um, I think I will have more to say about this, in certain respects, when the reading period comes. It was the land, of course, which I discovered, but as a young boy we lived at times, my father, and I and family, in the Pacific Northwest, Bremerton, Washington where my father was stationed in the naval station there. And he'd take me out into the hills and the creeks and rivers out in the Olympic Peninsula, and I fell in love with that country, that rainforest, and all of that. And I remember getting in the end of one summer stay there the news that we were going to move back to Washington, DC and I simply fell into bed crying. I hated that, to say goodbye to this land; and that Alaska, at that time [to me], was just a remote place. I had no idea that I might ever venture up there. But during the First World War my father was stationed briefly in Kodiak. I [have] forgotten the reasons why, but other things occurred, and after the war there were various benefits given to war veterans and the educational bill was one of them. But I hadn't really written about this, I don't think, there was an article written in the *Washington Post* one day back in 1946-47 announcing that the government was going to be offering free land to returning veterans in Alaska. And that started the fire. And I and others that I knew, we started talking about what we were going to do and so forth, and many just dropped off the program, so to speak, didn't go, but I knew this is what I wanted to do. I had no idea as to exactly what would become of it there; find a piece of land, settle down, and make a life. That was it. And the complications, of course, developed later on. I did come up the early summer of 1947 with a friend, who later left because he had a wife and child back in Washington. But we talked about getting the girls, the women, to come join us. Well, unfortunately, it didn't happen. My girlfriend took up with a, some student friend at George Washington University, but we stayed friends over the years, but it was a big disappointment. It was a fancy idea that these gals would come up there after we put up a cabin or two and we'd get together and make a life. So I spent that summer alone and my first winter and the following spring, and so forth, and went back to Washington and then New York to continue my art studies. In the meantime, I established the homestead and applied for what the government called a patent at that time, and it took several years [for] that.

But it was a long, long story and I can't go into all the details, but the land itself, when my time comes to read I will get off into a somewhat different aspect of things. Because I was fortunate in settling down in Richardson, an old gold rush community which is in Tenderfoot, and there were, still, some of the old timers there, and I got acquainted with them and they taught me a great deal. It was not just the land itself. There was a history behind it and the individuals there still left over from the gold rush era, and they taught me, and made a tremendous difference. I've written about it better than I can speak it right here. It was the matter of the land but not just the land. It was the history behind it; the people and what they left behind them, and so forth...

Question to laureates: Being in the silence. Is it harder to find the quiet center? Is solitude hard to find? What is your relationship to solitude? Is it harder to find in Alaska?

John Haines: You can find it anywhere, on a park bench somewhere.

Question to laureates: Is it harder for you to find solitude—or do you just go to a park bench?

John Haines: A lot of things of course have changed since I came up here, over the years, when I first came here. I may have something more to say when I read a little bit. I am more well aware, especially in the Fairbanks area that I knew as a small leftover gold mining town at that time, and then came the military expansion during the war. And the renovating and the highways and so forth—it has changed in a way that at times has even offended me. What had I come here for, where is it? But that partly is a disposition on my part. The land is still there and solitude, and what have you, is still there with it. Just depends on where you look and where you might go, you see, but there are other aspects of it, which I want to refer to when my reading time comes. And that remains important to me; and that concerns the people that I knew and who made a very big difference in my life. The old folks who taught me so much and it wouldn't have been the same without them. And they made a tremendous difference on the land when they came here. I learned for example, I looked out over the hills in Fairbanks when I first came there and the trees were all pretty small and not many big spruce or anything around there. During recent years, several decades, they have gone back up. But I have learned that the first settlers came in there, they had to burn wood, so they not only cut but they also set fire to the forest there to kiln the wood, to get it nice and dead, so they could get it for firewood and burn it. And that was a big surprise for me. When I first knew it, I had no idea what had gone on there; and around Richardson, where I settled, the same thing had happened. Now the spruce are coming back and I wish they hadn't done that. But those changes there and the imprint left on the land by people, at one time or another, that is part of it. And it's a mix[ed] business, perhaps. I would not dismiss the positive influence that many of these older people had on me. So I still remember, like, my early images of Fairbanks, and I wish it hadn't changed so much even though, at the time, there was a one block section of Second Avenue and another block section of Cushman St. that were paved. Everything else was gravel and dirt, which, you know, was kind of gritty in a way. But it made a difference.

Question to laureates: What are some of the stories, or the most urgent stories in Alaska now that we should be trying to tell?

John Haines: I want to say, thinking about land and our relationship to it, I spent most of a year in England on a scholarship from Harvard University, from the late 1970s and it was a very revealing experience for me. I'm Scots-Irish, Anglo-Irish ancestry for the most part, and I, to my surprise, I began to feel at home over there and to the extent that when I finally came back after that year was over, people remarked to me back in Fairbanks and elsewhere that "you talked like a Brit." And I miss but think about the landscape and Yorkshire, and spent most of the time in Scotland, Orkney Islands, of all the history and influx of people and tribes and so forth and the conflicts and so forth, left its mark on the land. But there is still there something that's very beautiful; it's just there, that imprint, and I felt the same thing in Northern Italy where I spent a month on a scholarship or fellowship, more recently, and there the Roman residue is also apparent. All that history adds to the land itself, in my opinion, it's not just landscape but our participation in landscape, what we have done and whether good or bad, the land always comes back. Get rid of humanity and everything will come back. There will be plenty of animals scrabbling over it. But that history, the land, what it means to us or can mean to us, it's not just nature, see—there is more than that, in my opinion.

Questions between laureates

Ann Hanley: What keeps you here?

John Haines: Ain't got no place to go.

Nancy Lord: If you were not primarily a writer, or partly a writer, what else would you be?

John Haines: I would have been an artist. I was very involved for several years in painting, drawing, and sculpture and so forth. I won a prize in sculpture, but I knew that I came into a conflict and I had a very strong memory. Once when I was in New York I was trying to decide what I was going to do, make a decision. And I was walking down the Lower East Side and was walking up to 8th Street in the Village and with school, and I stopped at a street corner, and it had happened that I was having trouble with migraine headaches. And I stood at that corner and decided that it was going to be poetry. And my headaches disappeared. But it was a difficult thing because I had the talent for the visual arts and I loved it. And I later got, became involved in photography, for example—but I made the decision and it was one of those fundamental things. If I had stayed with the visual arts, I would have had to stay in New York or Washington and some place to have access to art galleries and dealers and things like that, but it is true that if you are good enough and fortunate you can make money—your paintings and sculptures you can sell. You can't make any money selling a poem.

Richard Dauenhauer: A testimony and comment. I am glad that you decided on poetry and that your migraine went away because I think all of us grew up sort of under the overcoat of *Winter News*. And I think, to me, it was a real turning point in Alaska literature. I can't tell for how many of us, that was the first really new thing—the opening lines of *Winter News*. So, thank you very much for that, and I'm glad you had the insights.

John Haines: Well, I'd like to tell you a little story to close off before commenting. But I was in Washington studying art and was very much involved with studying writing, but my American University came to an end, and my father arranged for me to get a job as a statistical draftsman at the Department of Navy. I needed to make some money. And it was interesting, but I went to talk to the supervisor at the department I would be involved with. [He] had some minor papers and so forth and he saw my education and he said, he looks at me and says, "I see you've been studying art. We don't want any malcontents here." And I thought, what? Malcontent? And a short time later he looked at me and gave me back my papers and said, "Remember, we don't want any malcontents here." I never forgot that.

(Laughter in the room)

Questions from the audience

Walter Parker: When did you give up trapping?

John Haines: In the late '60s, my dogs died off and things were changing. The literary invitations were coming, and both my parents died in the late '60s, and life just changed in a certain way. And I figured it was the end of it. I didn't want to do that anymore. Things were changing, I don't know. But trapping was part of the life there for many years, but it wasn't going to be my life career, you see. It was part of the subsistence life. When, one winter, I came to town in Fairbanks with some marten fur that I had caught, and the fur, and so forth, I got $220, which was a lot of money to us then. That's the main reason that I did that, it was not that I enjoyed killing these animals, I know that. Especially a larger one like a lynx, for example, but it's part of the life that's one way of making some money, occasionally selling some fish, caught salmon under the Tanana and so forth. Couldn't pass that up. It wasn't just for the experience; I know it was part of the economy, what I could do. You did this?

Walter Parker: Oh yeah—stopped in 1964.

English Professor Suzanne Forster: How can we accept poetry in our culture as a way of knowing in our language? What is your intended tone in *Winter News*? How would you describe the tone in *Winter News*? Ominous or uplifting?

John Haines: The tone? I don't think I had that in mind at all, whether it was…I was trying to tell the truth about things, as I had experienced it.

But there was also all the influence of the time. First, from the Classical Chinese poetry, I learned to write very short poems condensed. Then I also began, there in the 1960s, reading poetry from Spanish and German poets, Modernist, and others as a movement that was taking place in the poetry world. And I learned from that. In one way or another, I was just...I had my life I had been living. I had to find ways to express that as well as I could. And at that time I was not writing prose or telling stories in prose but found that I needed to tell the story somehow and so in a few lines or sometimes in more than a few lines. But I had many, many samples, examples, from poetry in my memory from classical times to modern. And all of that had its influence. I don't know exactly how to answer that question. It was an activity that I pursued, so to speak, that when I could find time for it, with all the outside and outdoors work that I was doing consumed so much time, I found time to read but in late fall and early winter I could take time for my writing.

English Professor Suzanne Forster: Not a friendly snowman out there? And a student said I was reading into it.

John Haines: The poem "Winter News," well, it sounds pretty grim.

English Professor Suzanne Forster: Take my side.

John Haines: The poem, the poem was the second poem in *Winter News* after "If the Owl Calls Again," and well that was specifically anchored in an event at that time, in the winter of 1961-62, the coldest winter I ever saw here. It got to 70 below at the homestead. We got [a] brief account on the radio or somewhere, news that down in Northway and [in the] area there, they closed the schools, people were waiting for some warmth that finally came, a big chinook came, but everything just came to a stop. And that's what spurred me to write that poem. I heard the news that the children came home or were not going to school. I made up images for it. Don't ask me why I did it.

Readings from laureates

John Haines: Since someone has already mentioned it, I'll read from that poem "Winter News" and the comment that this goes back to the winter of 1961-62, the coldest I ever saw here, at minus 71 at the homestead for a couple of nights, then came a tremendous blast of warm air from the south that changed things. From minus 71 the next evening it was 10 above. It felt like summer.

WINTER NEWS

They say the wells
are freezing
at Northway where
the cold begins.

Oil tins bang
as evening comes on,
and clouds of
steaming breath drift
in the street.

Men go out to feed
the stiffening dogs,

the voice of the snowman
calls the white-
haired children home.

I mentioned, I think at one point here, I'm going to read a couple of those early poems, poems influenced by Classical Chinese poetry, that I began studying, so to speak, and it taught me a great deal, to write to condense whatever it was that I thought I had to say in very few lines. And I'll read a couple of those. Two poems after Li Po.

I—CONVERSATION

If you ask me why
I live here on
this lonely hillside,

I will smile and say:

the autumn leaves
drift on the moving
water, and
the world of men
is far away.

Uh, ha ha. That's the way I felt sometimes.

II—QUIET NIGHT

Moonlight spills
across the bed,
outside the frost
is deepening.

I lie awake and
watch the changing
shadows, thinking
of the lonely earth.

I'll read one more of these, "Untitled." My first wife Peggy was with me two years at the homestead, but Alaska was not for her; she wanted New York. And that's where she's been ever since. I visited her there; we stayed friends. I understood.

UNTITLED

I see you going down
a dusty road
in the amber light;

the sun is setting
and I close
the greenhouse door.

New vines will grow again
next summer, but you

will not come back.

And I'm going to read here a section of prose from a chapter called "With an Axe and an Auger" from this particular section of *The Stars, The Snow, The Fire*. I discuss the people I knew at the time, mostly men. And as I think I mentioned in earlier comments so far this evening, it's not just the land itself but the people I knew and met and the imprints that anywhere I went there were these signs of earlier settlers who were there, one time or another, and what they left behind there. The land was pretty well emptied when I came to it. And mostly I think it still is. That was important to me, as I mention in this brief section I'm going to read, it's a... they were friends and teachers, and I learned a great deal from them. One of the old timers there, Billy Melvin, of whom I have written and specifically discussed, discussed the early days. There was a mixed feeling from some of the early settlers there about the Native people and for the most [part] they respected them. I hadn't heard a [any] word from them, but he heard one guy talking about some natives in a negative way and he came up to him and said, "You don't talk that way, those people are just as good as you are." And he meant it. It was things like that that made an impression on me. So, I'll read this.

WITH AN AXE AND AN AUGER, IV

The land lives in its people. It is more alive because they worked it, because they left this hillside and that creek bottom marked by their shovels and axes. The meaning of this place lies in the rough weight of their hands, in the imprint of their gum-booted travel.

Here among the willows you will find old pipe fittings, valves, and chunks of steam hose; they are scattered with rusty tins, bent hoops and splintered boxes. In this place, Ike Isaacson sank his prospect hole and fired his boiler. His cabin has fallen to rot and rain, but for those of us who remember, this tangled blueberry flat is still Ike's bench.

Up there where the woods are thinned, someone whose name has escaped all memory built his cache and hung up his winter's meat. Lying there, half-sunken in the moss, are the hewn and punky timbers, and here in the living spruce a rusty spike has gathered a knot of pitch.

And on this sandy knoll, someone else we knew had a cabin. Here were the fence posts of his garden. And look, a few woody stalks of rhubarb still break through the sod by the corner post each spring.

At this bend in the road, not far from the fallen bridge, Melvin killed his grizzly with a pistol.

They are useful ghosts, these old inhabitants with their handwork implements, their settled lives. They tell us something of what we have been, and if we live long enough and well enough, what each of us may become: one more sign of our residence on earth, alive by reason of remembered love.

I was lucky to have known them when I did, for they are no longer standing in their patched wool and mended cotton. In some way I have always accepted, they were my people, if the phrase now means anything, and the best of them I have loved with a deep appreciation that has never left me. They were friends and teachers, and I do not expect to see their kind again.

When I think of them now, it is of something hugely tender and forgiving, akin to a healing thingness in the world that assures the soil of its grasses, the earth of its sun.

They are voices, gestures, faces peering out of old photographs, but not that only. They live as names spoken from the shadows: Campbell, Melvin, Hershberger, Doherty, Fry. There were some, like Kievic and Sam Loma, who died before I came; I knew them only as figures looming half legendary in the local stories.

The cemetery site at Richardson long ago caved into the Tanana; it is silt and driftwood with the rest of the riverbed. On a slope outside Fairbanks, intergrown with birches, with mosses and strawberry vines, the glass-covered nameplates are cracked and muddied, their letters erased by the weather. No doubt they are all recorded in some basement file in the courthouse, written down with the deeds and taxes in a musty ledger.

But the people live in these hills, in the shape of their ditches, their mounds and cellars. They are accounted for in the names they gave to the country, to its furrows and pockets, its upraised bones; a hidden lake, a creek like so many others, one windy dome among a hundred ridges. I know of more than one high tributary named in passing by a man reminded of the place he came from; amused or forgetful, inventing as he walked, or moved perhaps by something in the far-off news of that day: *Empire, Republican, Buckeye, Carrie Nation.*

A wandering spirit came home to the land. In the shape of a man, it cleared a space in the forest and built a shelter from the trees at hand. It came to learn the ways of this country; to sleep and awaken, to flourish and grow old; to watch the river, the clouds moving east, the frost in the grass.

It will never die completely. Look for it in the trails you follow, in the amber blazes on black bark. You will find it in the settled forge, in the rotting windlass, in the cabin sill you come upon by a creek that has no name, in the green scar on that far hill.

THREE POEMS

John Haines Stacking Wood, Richardson, June 1987 *(William Stafford Collection: Stafford Photo Exhibit 2014, #65; photograph by William Stafford reprinted by permission of the Estate of William Stafford)*

This is a photograph of John Haines' literary birthplace where his life as poet began. A peaceful, idyllic scene of physical work done at the homestead.

The following poems offer insights into what John Haines learned from Richardson. They encircle moments of an individual and solitary awareness that, through the art of poetry, can be recognized and shared by others.

INTO THE GLACIER

With the green lamp of the spirit
of sleeping water
taking us by the hand...

Deeper and deeper,
a luminous blackness opening
like the wings of a raven—

as though a heavy wind
were rising through all the houses
we ever lived in—

the cold rushing in,
our blankets flying away
into the darkness,
and we, naked and alone,
awakening forever...

POEM

The immense sadness
of approaching winter
hangs in the air
this cloudy September.

Today a muddy road
filled with leaves, tomorrow
the stiffening earth and
a footprint
glazed with ice.

The sun breaking through
still warm, but the road
deep in shadow;
your hand in mine is cold.

Our berries picked,
the mushrooms gathered,
each of us hides
in his heart a small piece
of this summer,
as mice store their roots
in a place
known only to them.

We believe in the life to come,
when the stark tree
stands in silence above
the blackened leaf;
but now at a bend in the road
to stop and listen:

strange song
of a southbound bird
overflows
in the quiet dusk
from the top
        of that tree.

IN THE FOREST WITHOUT LEAVES XII

In all the forest, chilled
by its spent wealth,

in the killed kingdom of grass
where birch leaves
tumble and blow;

(and over the leaves is written:
how great the harvest,
how deep the plow)

I know one truth:

Nothing stains like blood,
nothing whitens like snow.

"DEAR RACHEL," LETTERS 2009-2011

The exchange of letters and cards created a special type of relationship and friendship. I wanted John to be in the present, even with his recollections of younger days. To be in the present not the past. Old age, being alone, wondering what one can share when dependent for basic care, was the stark reality he faced.

While corresponding with John Haines, I did not preserve what I wrote because the act of writing was not self-conscious, or something written to be critiqued. To show John Haines' lighthearted side, texts of selected greeting cards have been included. Sections of letters that were overly personal have been excluded with ellipses.

Rachel Epstein

Correspondence 2009

From: John Haines [...]
Sent: Sunday, March 15, 2009 2:05 PM
To: RACHEL EPSTEIN

Subject: Re: Just Checking

John,

Have you gotten your ticket?

Rachel, just to be certain, I want you to know my mailing address. It is now: 611 Sandpiper Dr. Fairbanks 99709. I had been using a university PO address but that is no longer possible. Please let me know if I should send you a copy of my flight ticket.

John Haines

ଛଈ

611 Sandpiper Dr.
Fairbanks, AK 99709

16 March 2009

Rachel Epstein
UAA Bookstore
Anchorage 99508

Dear Rachel,

Here is a copy of my ticket/itinerary for the coming April event. If for some reason there are any changes, I'll let you know, but I doubt there will be any to cope with.

One thing of importance is the change in my Fairbanks address, due to some university policy I had not been aware of, I cannot receive personal mail through the campus postal service. So, as you will see on the envelope and above, I will not get my mail at my house address. I should have corrected this while visiting with the travel agent, but it was still not clear to me at the time what I was having to deal with. Phone and mail remain the same, at least at this time.

I look forward to seeing you at the airport. Thank you for your service!

Best regards,
John Haines

ಊ

[ENCLOSED NOTECARD]

SMACK of JELLYFISH

Sarah Asper-Smith

Did you know?
The Arctic Tern has the longest migration route of any bird,
traveling up to 22,000 miles.
These birds live up to 30 years.
Because Arctic Terns travel from Arctic to the Antarctic,
they experience the most amount of daylight possible!

If you were an Arctic tern…
I would fly to the ends of the earth to be with you.

[In John's handwriting:]
Well,
I'm an Arctic Loon! But I'd
Still come looking for you!
      John

                                                    8 April 09

Dear Rachel,

    It was a real treat to spend time with you last week, and I remain very grateful for your companionship at the airport and elsewhere during that brief time. I hope to see you again, but who knows when or where?

    I think you mentioned the German Weimar Republic during one of our conversations. I have a very hefty hardback copy of a book on that postwar period, with many pictures of the persons involved, and the artwork produced at the time.

    But I want to mention also, if I didn't, the life and work of Rosa Luxemburg who was very active during that period, an avid supporter of the republic. [See Notes in Appendix] Alas, she and her colleague Karl Liebnicht, were murdered by the state police in January 1919. I have a copy of her letters, and I have read them many times. But I want to tell you that there is a film, in German of course, on the life and fate of Rosa. I have seen it more than once, and I will hope to watch it again. It is it is not available on DVD, but the university library has it here in the older VHS form. You might look for it in the UAA library; it's worth it, and I think you'll find it worth watching and thinking about.

    Well, I'm a student of that period, and much of the time and events that followed. Rosa was Jewish, by the way, another reason for you to seek it out. I hope they get it into the DVD form; it belongs there.

    So, I hope to hear from you. Thank you again for being there last week.

      Love,
      John

24 April 09

Dear Rachel,

Thank you for the card and letter, so good to have, and I will try to respond to at least some of what you had to say and ask about. However, I want first of all to pass on these few pages from the book on Weimar Germany.* I have gone back to it since my trip to Anchorage and our conversation on this and that, and since Rosa Luxemburg was a part of all this. I thought you might find these pages worth a look. The book itself has been something I've returned to now and then, if only to look at the many illustrations and photographs of persons and works of art from the period. As I think I said, it is a hefty book, and not something to leaf through in a hurry.

I have read some of Ingeborg Bachmann, [Austrian poet, 1926-1973] but have not seen work by the other writer you mention. I have trouble reading his last name; it looks like: Pi29link! [Alejandra Pizarnik, Argentinian poet, 1936-1972] Now, what the hell is that? You tell me, Madam Epstein. I also have not read the work by Kandinsky you mention, but will look for it in the UAF library.

As for what I am doing, I have been reading this and that, replying to the many letters I get from friends, paying some bills, and waiting for the bad news of my income tax, a complicated matter I turn over to a friend and agent here. I shiver to think of what I may have to pay. If it turns out to be as bad as I expect, I may turn to the Hemlock solution and bid the whole damned thing farewell!

I expect to be back in Anchorage briefly on June 28 and 29, for a meeting of the United States Artists, an organization that awarded me a very generous check for my many years of writing. I will be with my good friend, John L. Adams who also received one of their fellowships in 2006. It will be brief, and we will be housed in one of the major hotels downtown, the Hilton. You might check this out, and if there is time for it, you could stop off for a visit, or maybe attend the meeting they plan to have. I can't say more than that, and the time will be short: two days and two nights, and the 29th is my birthday! June 29, 1924. An odd coincidence.

As for what I want, as you say it, I want a place to retire, and some time left in which to complete a few unfinished writings, etc. And then: I want some peace and quiet! Farewell, my friends and enemies! I will leave you my rented Ford Fuckus, and may you please pay the bills!

Thank you again Rachel, and don't hesitate to write to me anytime you wish. I hope we can meet once more…

Love,
John

I liked reading your brief German sentence, or quote, from Heine.

From my great pains,
I make my tiny songs

Aus meinen grossen schmerzen
Mach ich die kleinen Lieder

*Letter included a copy of the cover and first chapter of Eric D. Weitz' book, W*eimar Germany: Promise and Tragedy,* Princeton University Press.

3 May 09

Dear Rachel,

Thank you for the letter and your good news, re "Rosa" and the Weimar book: they fit together, as I'm sure you know by now. I'm so glad you and Kathy Tarr were able to watch the film together, and I am damned glad I told you about it. Not many people now know of Rosa Luxemburg and the Weimar period, and I wish the film were available in DVD. Perhaps if a few of us asked for it, demanded it, maybe the film company would produce it. Time for it to happen, I say.

I want to mention another film you may not have seen or heard of, and another book, or two, from that period which I have seen or read, and come to value immensely.

The film, Sophie Scholl, is not well known or viewed by many. I discovered it in a video store here, rented it, and then bought a copy for my own. It is a true story, as is Rosa's, though it takes place in the early years of WWII, and is about a group of young German university students in Munich who joined in a movement they called "The White Rose," who worked to post various papers and other resistance material in opposition to the Nazi party and its policies. Sadly, Sophie, her brother and a friend, were arrested and executed (as might be expected, alas). But you should be able to find it in a local Blockbuster or some other store.

That said, there is a book you might want to read, and which I bought a copy of after reading a review of it. The title: Resistance, by Agnes Humbert. Again, it is documentary, a true story of Agnes and other women who worked (while under arrest) to free women and others who were put to work by the German occupation of France, many of whom were simply killed when they became too ill and weak to work. But Agnes survived and was honored for her work. I read the story from page to page until the very end of it; something I had not known of before. It does pay, me at least, to read reviews from time to time!

I can't imagine you have not read or heard of Irene Nemirovsky's Suite Francaise. When I saw a notice of it in one of the journals or papers I subscribe to, I knew I wanted that book, and when I got it, I more or less lived in it, reading a few pages at a time, morning and evening. I felt myself a part of Irene's life, its time and place, and on finishing the book,

I sought and bought everything about her writing available in English, including a fine biography of her and family by Jonathan Weiss.

So, enough of my reading history for the moment, I will enclose here a copy of a page on the "resistance" people throughout much of Europe during that period who in one way or another worked to free the prisoners, the slaves and victims of that human disaster, of which we Americans truly know all too little.

Now, as for old Ezra [Ezra Pound, 1885-1972], he was a teacher for me in my early years as poet, he and Williams [William Carlos Williams, 1883-1963], Eliot [T.S. Eliot, 1888-1965], and others. I was only marginally aware of his apparently Fascist sympathies. When I learned of it, I think I stopped reading him for a while. When I was living in DC after the war, engaged in my art studies, and later at work in the Navy Dept. in order to earn some money, I learned of Pound's detention in St. Elizabeth's Hospital. I even thought of trying to pay him a visit, were it possible. It wasn't, of course. But there is always some measure of forgiveness, and for me Ezra Pound remains an important figure in modern American and European Letters.

So, there you have it. I may have more to say before I send this off tomorrow.

I found a copy of the page I mentioned of German resistance during WW II, and here it is. I took it from a special V-Day issue of Time Magazine in which I found many, many photos and accounts of that war and its closing episodes, and I like sharing some of this with friends who might find them worth [a] look and a listen! Not the stuff of major news, unfortunately, but sometimes we are lucky to find a page like this, and others I have come upon from time to time. I, of course, a veteran and with a strong historical sense, never quit looking and saving! It's my history also, and I ain't gonna give up on it.

I would like to see someone make a film based on Suite Francaise. Maybe it will happen, and it should.

Give my best wishes to Kathy Tarr. Thank you again for writing, and for keeping me in mind (or maybe heart?), and you will always be here in mine!

Love,
John

I loved getting your recent card and envelope. When I first saw it, I thought: Hmmm…looks as if it fell into a snow puddle somewhere. But it was/is a pleasure to have something like this in the mail. You do write well, and I have no trouble reading you. So, let the poor old elephant keep on browsing!

༄

[ENCLOSED NOTECARD]

Madison Park Greetings, Inc.
Shannon Martin/Girl Designer 2007

"IF YOU CAN SPEND A PERFECTLY USELESS AFTERNOON IN A PERFECTLY USELESS MANNER, YOU HAVE LEARNED HOW TO LIVE"
Lin Yutang

[In John's handwriting:]
When?
Could we find a patch of
grass and a nice blanket
to lie on? Hmm…I'd like
that!
  John

14 May 09

Rachel,

Thank you once more for the card and the good handwriting. I don't want to burden you with another long letter and depressing suggestions re Wartime and revived histories, etc. As for my suicide solution, well, I almost typed my address as: 611 Hemlock! ain't kidding...ahem! But don't let it worry you, if it does; I am not about to make any decisions on that issue.

But to be brief, you mention Pound and your B-day. When was that? He was born in 1885, but I don't know the day and hour! Yours? I'd like to know.

But since you mentioned Uncle Ezra, I have been reminded, and in a good way, of his mentorship of me as a young poet, how much it meant to read his essays and early poems. This morning I took out a recent anthology and read once more his bio and some of the poems I loved when young. They are still good to read, and my rereading may help revive my presently sagging creative energies.

So, thanks once more for your thoughts and writing. I have learned, incidentally, that I will be in Anchorage until late afternoon on the 30th, and with free time. My flight will leave at 4:20. So, if possible I would love to see you again, perhaps have a brief lunch, or something. But it is up to you. Plenty of time ahead.

Love,
John

8 June 09

Dear Rachel,

I apologize for being so tardy in responding to your good letter of last month...

I was glad to hear you are, or were, reading Suite Francaise; I'd like to hear what you think of it. I can imagine a great film being made of it, or some parts of it. Amazing, to me, that the book sat for sixty years in a duffle bag belonging to the older daughter, Denise, she being afraid to take it out and read it. And then, in a short time not long ago, the story [was] edited and published. Something of a miracle, I say.

You were born in San Diego, you say. You must remember Coronado across the bay, where I lived as a boy during the 1930s and early '40s. My father was stationed in the area, and we loved living there when possible. [See Notes in Appendix] My brother lives there with his wife and family, and my mother died there in the late 1960s. I was in my senior year at Coronado High School when I was drafted in 1943 and sent over to the SD Naval Training Station; and from there, later, out into the S Pacific and into the war. When were you last there?

I never heard, or read, of the Pound incident you mention, but it does sound like something Ezra might come up with. Too bad he ain't still here; he might have some witty ideas for getting Americans out of Iraq. Well, maybe a toadstool on Obama's plate!

As for Sexton, 69 years sounds pretty young to me at this time. I often wish I were 65 again. Now, you were born in 1956, which brings you to the age of 53—right? Pretty young, gal, you with all them cats you mention. I'll bring a blanket if you got some good grass to lie on. No need to get up, just snooze in the sun with a kitty for company!

Well, I love getting your letters, Rachel; you write well, and with good thought behind the words. Have you anything in verse or prose

I might read? Or perhaps you mentioned this when we were together in April. I do look forward to seeing you again, and will do my best to make some time for us to talk a bit, and so forth. As your dear Woodrat friend, I send my love and regards, always.

 John

---

                         13 June 09

Dear Rachel,

 Just a short note to thank you for the email yesterday, and to ask you to print it out and send me a copy. I have not the means to do this, and I want very much to be able to read the printed copy and return to it. This is especially important to me with our new friendship, and I dislike the thought of things disappearing on the touch of a computer key!

 I went with a friend here to my old homestead 68 miles south of Fairbanks. It is always deeply moving for me to be back there, and at times also saddening to see the neglect and deterioration of things. But my friend and I did some work, and hauled away in his truck a stack of stuff: scraps and discarded roofing tin, things that a group of UAF students left behind when they were out there a couple of years ago. And then the drive back to Fairbanks, past the Airforce base and into old junktown USA. I so love it out there, I think sometimes of going out with a dose of Hemlock, choosing a place to sleep, and so: Goodbye! But not yet.

 I look forward to seeing you again, and Kathy also.

 Love,
 John

❦

From: John Haines [...]
Sent: Tuesday, June 16, 2009 1:45 PM
To: RACHEL EPSTEIN
Subject: RE: Hello Out There

Rachel, I just had word from USA that they will pay for an extra night for me if I choose to stay on in order to meet with you. So, keep that in mind. I also asked them about having someone meet/us at the airport on the 28. Will let you know about that. Well, you have me, whether or not you need me! Love, John. Also, would you print your previous email and send me the copy? I can't do it, and I like to keep track of what you may have to say to me, etc. I like paper!

❦

24 June 09

Dear Rachel,

    You may get this brief letter and enclosures in time for our meeting down there this coming weekend. I thought you might find the letter from USA interesting, and on a recent rereading I saw mention of my bringing a guest to the dinner...a thought anyway, if it can be done and you would be willing or able to attend! Otherwise, we will make time for it on the 30th. I am still attempting to confirm our Anchorage arrival time on the 28th, but my friend Adams is still out of town, and I'll hope to talk to him before the time closes in. If I get it, I'll call and let you know. I'm sure we can get a cab to the hotel if you can't make it, or it may be that Adams has arranged for a ride from one of his friends down there.

The other item I've enclosed is for your amusement (I hope!), and not intended as a seduction. As you can see, I wrote it many years ago, and I still can't remember what may have prompted me to write it... possibly something I had been reading? Or I was just in a naughty mood. I was living in California at the time, but getting ready to return to Alaska and the homestead. We were then in the Monterey area, perhaps in Carmel Valley. Anyway, I was doing a lot of reading and working on many of my immature poems, a few of which have since been collected in a small book by Copper Canyon Press [*At the End of This Summer, Poems 1948-1954*]. I hope you can at least get a laugh from it, and share it with Kathy Tarr.

My new prose collection [*Descent*] is now with the press back east, after a lot of labor on my part, and I hope things will now come together and the book be published early next year. I am relieved to be done with it, or most of it, and can now turn my attention to a few new projects in verse and prose, or just sit back and read a while, and catch up with some long-awaiting correspondence. I'm very glad, by the way, that you got to read my War Memoir and had such good words to say for it. Thank you, my dear new friend, soon to be an old one!?

Well, as I think I have said in one way or another, you are, have been, a gift, and there is nothing wrong with Love...I have it, and you have it—forever!

John

THE HORNY SHEPHERD TO HIS LOVE

To hell with it, dear!
I'd have you standing
like a rosy ass
    on a hilltop,
prefiguring the sun,
    to light my days.

Your sturdy flanks,
how they quiver! Your arms—
to the bushes, love!
    Up there, away
from this drainage ditch...
    Come on, shy lady!

What does it matter
if the greasy flocks complain
of the shepherd's neglect?
    So long as we are
safe and warm, let
    the damned things bleat!

Listen to the starving crows!
Melodious songs, indeed!
Foolish poets,
    to make a pastoral
blessing of that!
    What a silly thought!

Sure, I'll make you
a girdle—or rather, I'll…
Yes, yes, and posies
    too—I know,
I won't forget.
    Ah, here we are!

Ouch! these brambles
prick—spread out your cloak.
And now to work—
    Oh, let the wolves

take them! Hah,
    the shepherd's life!

    John Haines,
    1953

From: John Haines [...]
Sent: Wednesday, June 24, 2009 2:00 PM
To: RACHEL EPSTEIN
Subject:

Rachel, a letter in the mail for you, with a couple of items you may find worth reading. Time gets short, and I hope to send you an arrival time in ANC soon. Rain and cold here, but at least it ain't frost!
    Love,
    John

From: John Haines
Sent: Friday, June 26, 2009 1:12 PM
To: RACHEL EPSTEIN
Subject: RE:

Rachel, Adams and I spend time together here, and we will on the flight, so don't let that concern you. He'll understand my need to spend some time with you, and he has other folks there he will want to see. So, don't let this affect you! *John*

ه‌و

From: John Haines [...]
Sent: Friday, June 26, 2009 1:28 PM
To: RACHEL EPSTEIN
Subject: RE: Visit

Rachel, I forgot to say that you are right! I haven't changed much since I wrote that naughty verse ...

ه‌و

8 July 09

Dear Rachel,

I just recently sent a note and with a copy of my UA DUNCIAD, which I think I recited a few lines from while we were together, you and I and Kathy. Anyway, you can share it with her when the time comes.

The Spanish poem I may have recited from was not from a Cuban poet but a famous Spanish classic: "Copias por la Muerte de su Padre" from Jorge Manrique (1440-1479). [See Notes in Appendix] Actually,

15th century. You can find this poem as well as many others among the Spanish classics in The Penguin Book of Spanish Poetry, ed. by J.M. Cohen. The first edition, the one I learned from, was published in 1956. The one I have with me here is the latest edition, 1988. The text, contents, etc., are the same. You might find a copy of it in the university library or have the bookstore order a copy.

Your asking me about this reminds me that I sent the information and a copy of a page or two, to Amada Cruz, one of the USA people who was there and with whom I discussed this poem. She herself is Espanola; her husband is from Cuba. Incidentally, in Spanish you don't pronounce it like Key-u-ba, but as Cooba. In any case, Manrique's poem, on the death of his father, was the one poem he wrote, and one of the great poems in Spanish Lt.

So, that's it, Rachel. Think about it: write one great poem! That's all it takes, and nevermind this MFA junk published in our time!

And, yes, too bad we didn't have more time together, but that's how it was, is, at an event like that USA meeting, and my b-day thrown in with it. But I'll see you again, if not here on Earth, then in Heaven when the time comes!

Love,
John

PS: The two author names for my Dunciad, Bernard Meade, are in fact my two middle names, inherited from my father, and from my school days as a Catholic kid. I don't remember Latin verses from my school days.

And I did send my brother a copy of a War Memoir, I'm certain of that, though I can't recall any response from him.

As for the "Haines Group," you can write to a friend, Miles Moore, who keeps track of these things.

He's a very good friend, former student at GWU, and a good writer.

THE UA DUNCIAD
SOME MOCK-HEROICS ON A RENEWABLE THEME
by Bernard Meade

Dedicated to Messrs Dunham & Sexton,
and to all those desiring a portion
of Truth in these parlous times.

And with additional homage to the
venerable firm of Pope & Dryden,
for their edifying example.

Printed in Helena, Montana, 1998

Of UAF its villains great and small,
On whom the legislative ashes fall—
Sing! O Muse (or snicker up your sleeve)
Of covert deans and why the students leave.

Of Waddle, bold, outrageous in her craft,
Who thinks a dog-run shuts out winter's draft!
Thus Whacker shreds the files and does not hear
The truth that cries beneath the paper tear.

With Merry stabbed and shamefully led astray,
Let Piggy smile to think she has her way—
We know the truth, and she must therefore lie
Who fakes an art and cannot tell us why.

Two honest men at least must here be named,
If matters worsen they shall not be blamed.
To speak one's mind, and let that thought be heard:
How seldom in the ranks has this occurred!

But see how Strutton strains his classroom fetters,
To pour such learned venom on his betters!
And Bard, who'd roundly censure at our need
A phony greatness sold by Random Weed!

Let Moron squeak, let politics prevail!
Where Justice faints, all values are for sale.
Let Envy rule the day, as Envy can—
He who praises to his class a man

He slanders on the sly may tenure make,
But honest colleagues know too well a fake…
Know well another joke, if somewhat slighter:
How Snoose without a book can be a writer!

Now let my list of Gumps grow short and meaner,
With Shrinkum, Fussy, O'Duck, and dull Skulweener…
What greatness, pray, when colleagues much like these
Would force a common high school to its knees?

Smaller and small bleat the coward crew,
To steer their college vessel in the stew—
The craft of Learning high on the fiscal rocks,
And, lo! asleep at the helm, Dementia Haycox!

Long in coming, always present, looms
This late accounting: Oft, in the chancellor rooms
And vacant chairs so much non-thought sits brewing
An ever—skiddy system's slow undoing.

From school to stool the regents scratch and ponder.
The profs retire, the adjuncts wince—small wonder

If our overpaid elects behave so fickle
In a state o'er run by wits like Holly Wickell

At UA southward Spurts will shift and sway—
A whiner, yes, but crafty in his way—
To float his program in a pool of small bed-wetters,
And so bring down this ailing art of Letters!

Poor Sackston, now retired, must fume in vain
To think the man he hired can still remain,
To weep and wink, contrive against all hopes,
His academic lineage out of Snopes!

From north to south, then back to north—what campus
Most deserves this stale and tawdry rumpus?
Why seek in so much twaddle, to learn in class
How small a thing it is to be an ass!

But Fairbanks is our aim, let Anchorage be,
With pity for all those who Outside flee
To find a school, a life, some useful work—
Or else stay on, be tutored by a jerk!

And now the wintry drafts come sifting down
On classroom, office, dorm, and blinkered town.
In Signers Hall the founders' spirit sours,
And somewhere in the murk Shrewmaker cowers.

The heat shut down, and sewage in the pool—
So knowledge flees and seeks another school.
The students who remain are UAF'd,
And blank confusion falls on all that's left!

Finis

MAY THE OWL CALL AGAIN

☙

18 July 09

Dear Rachel,

I haven't a decent card on hand here, but I wanted to respond briefly to yours which came here today, and a very rich thing it is, a nice surprise.

But you didn't make any mention of the UAF verses I sent you; I hope they didn't fall out of my envelope! I hope also that they gave you, and Kathy, some amusement. I hope to hear something from you on this.

A "Haines Group" in Alaska, or in Anchorage, etc., would have a difficult time, I think, with all the academic and laureate jealousies prevalent in the state. It's a nice idea, and I thank you for it, but... The group in DC and area are a different lot. They are not academic candidates for an MFA nor tenured university personae. They were all members of my classes at George Washington U. in 1991-92, but for the most part were working class folks who were able to attend my once-a-week evening class/workshop, discussion group. The rest of the week of teaching was given to various undergrad classes, and I can't remember one name from those two semesters. Unusual, but a fact. My other group of older people had a background in law and business, government work, and so-forth. That made the essential difference, and they were open to what I had to say on various topics, and the various texts I gave them to read and respond to.

So, if you follow through on this idea, keep in mind what I've had to say here, and maybe find a few interested people outside the university circle, or maybe a few janitors and dishwashers, launderettes, etc.

Which reminds me to mention a book I may have referred to before, and which I have been reading page by page and day by day: <u>The Other America</u>, by Michael Harrington. Originally published in 1962, and most recently in 1981. The edition I have been reading from was published in 1997 by Touchstone. It's available, and you should not have any trouble finding it if this interests you. The "Other America" is the population of poverty, far more prevalent than most of us realize. But I won't attempt to summarize what Harrington has to say. It's a great book, one I had not heard of but read about in a piece in the <u>Times Book Review</u> earlier this month.

So, my dear potential CEO, thank you for your attention to what I've had to say here, and for your apparent devotion to my writing. It was nice to hear of your reading of my "America"! Not many will have read that poem nor given it the thought you seem to have given it. Thank you, dear Rachel; I am grateful to have readers like you…Please stay in touch, and I will also.

Love,
John

PS: It's too bad, Rachel, that you are not closer. I may have one more semester class here this fall, and you would be welcome to sit in on it, as others have from time to time. Mostly, the students are undergrads and part of the university Honors Program. We meet once a week, late afternoon, and my basic procedure is to hand out various materials, on literature, poetics, social issues, etc., and they are to respond to these pieces in whatever way they are capable of. As I often say: I am giving you something to think about! And that's it!

༄

27 July 09

Dear Rachel,
...I am surprised also and more than pleased to learn that you know the Harrington book. Not many do, I can imagine, but it has

been a revelation for me. I still have a chapter to finish, and will do so, slowly...

...So, another book on the way, or so it looks, and maybe another after that: some poems, perhaps. I have a few so far uncollected but published in one journal or another.

I did like the two Chinese poems, by the way. They remind me of those I read and learned from back in the late 1950s and early '60s, a real lesson I needed at the time.

And I was very glad to hear that you think so well of my "America." I may have said this in a previous note. I am cheered by your apparent appreciation of my work, whether in verse or prose. Having you and Kathy down there has been a new thing for me, having been pretty well rejected by... and his ilk. I seem always to be a threat to certain folks, and that element still remains here in the UAF English Dept., though there is no possibility of me being hired to teach at this late time...

...Thanks again for the card and writing. I will stay in touch, and you can count on that.

 Love,
 John

The whiskey and the wine are here, delivered yesterday by Michelle. I haven't drunk any of it yet, but the bottles are nice to look at. I may wait for someone to share it with.

6 Aug 09

Dear Rachel,

Since we both have referred to poverty in this country and Harrington's great book on the subject, I thought I might send you a copy of a memoir essay I wrote a few years ago and which will be included in this new book I am waiting for. I don't think I need say anything about it, as the piece itself tells the story pretty well. I will be curious to hear what you think of it, but no rush to respond. You can pass it on to Kathy if you would like to, but that is up to you...

...I always love hearing from you, Rachel, whether card or letter, and I hope not to lose touch as the days and months get on and, for me, the years also...

...And, truth to tell, your friendship, new as it is, has been a real gift to me at this time, and I wish we were closer in terms of city and region, etc. I'm glad you are a writer, a letter-writer; not many are these years. An email, and for many that's it! But I want a piece of paper in my hand, and the warmth [of] a pen in another hand, "Faraway So Close..." to echo the title of a German film that I love.

So, please feel free to write to me whenever you want to or have something to tell me or respond to from something of mine. Hard to say how much longer I'll be around, but as long as I am, I will cherish your presence in my life.

Love
John

PS: I know of Sebald [W.G. Sebald, 1944-2001, German author of *The Rings of Saturn*], but I can't recall having read anything of his. Which reminds me to ask: did you finish reading Suite Francaise, and did you like it? Ever read Hermann Broch [Austrian writer, 1886-1952, author of *The Sleepwalkers*] or Robert Musil [Austrian writer, 1880-1942, author of the unfinished novel *The Man Without Qualities*]? Two writers whose work opened a new world of Letters for me in the early 1980s.

If you ever write anything of your own, Rachel, I'd love to see it—not as critic, but simply as reader!

As I'm sure you know from the news, it has been very unpleasant here this week: smoke, cloudy and dark, and at times pretty stinky. A little rain yesterday has helped, and I hope to see more. But just in case, don't use the outhouse; stay indoors and do your thing!

7 pp
2500 words

ON THE STREET

I have never been a Street person, someone for whom the street, the doorway, the alley corner, is home for a prolonged period. During my early days in Fairbanks in the summer of 1947, I often slept in the back of a truck I owned while parked downtown on Second Avenue, and waking at times to the sound of traffic, to closing doors, and to voices on the street in the long summer twilight. Then too I often camped by the roadside outside of town, with a makeshift tent set up, and a small woodstove, while I searched the nearby country for that piece of land I had come to find and settle.

And there was a day in August during that first summer when, no longer with a car or truck of my own, I walked nearly thirty miles from my campsite at Richardson toward Fairbanks before I finally caught a ride. I stopped briefly for coffee at one of the roadhouses where I approached an older couple on their way into town and asked them for a ride. They took a quick, sideways look at my rough clothing, my probably unshaven face, and refused me. In the long, footsore hours that followed I felt at times like an itinerant hobo on the road to nowhere. An occasional incident like this, however, was something I took in stride as being in the nature of things at the time, part of the adventure I had set out on in that early postwar period.

But once or twice in my life at a latter time I came close enough to understand something of that state of things, of utter homelessness: nowhere to go, no means of getting there. In late August of 1948, when I had returned to Washington from my first year and a half in Alaska and was re-entering school to continue my art studies, I rented a small top floor room on N Street, not far from Connecticut Avenue. In the dense late summer heat it was difficult to sleep in that room, and for a night or two I took my blanket and pillow and went into the park area on Dupont Circle to spend the night in what breeze there was at the time, and as I had recently seen others do. The streets were safe then as they are not now, and I found myself in a kind of neighborhood of like-minded people: men, women and children, most of them had homes to go to, but in those days before air-conditioning they were drawn out into the fresh air of the open park. Some were sleeping on the benches, others on the grass, and many of them engaged in conversation until late in the evening. I remember talking with a couple of friendly older men about my recent venture to the far North and what I had done there.

The days and nights gradually cooled, and I was soon taken up with school, with classes and studio work at American University, and no longer needed to sleep in the park. My situation then was not dire, though I was poor enough with my GI allowance, barely able to pay the monthly rent of $25, to buy my meals and art supplies, and an occasional book. To be poor, as student, as an artist, was at the time very much in the bohemian tradition, and I was not alone in my circumstances.

In early January of 1950, having finished a year of study in painting and sculpture at American U., and a period of work as a draftsman at the Navy Department, I moved to New York to continue my art studies. I was immediately and radically introduced to the Lower East Side of Manhattan, to the Bowery under Third Avenue EL, and to a poverty encountered daily on my walks to Hans Hofmann's School on Eighth Street in the Village. This was still at the time a neighborhood where the handcarts and horse wagons were common on nearby Rivington Street, with the block-long City Market flourishing not far away on Houston Street—a New York long since vanished.

It was during those first weeks in New York that I became aware of the worst of that homelessness: the men, and sometimes the women, camped by a blazing trash can, with the elevated train rumbling overhead, their hands held out for anything you might be willing to give, whether a coin or slice of bread. My fellow student and room-mate, Felix, who had moved to New York from Washington two years previously, knew better than I how to push them aside, and in truth we had nothing to give them. I was appalled, not having seen anything like it in my relatively safe and harbored childhood, though I had glimpsed as a boy, in the 1930s, the unemployed men and women in Southeast Washington, staring from the steps of rundown houses as we drove by. And I had, more recently, seen a war from the decks of a Navy destroyer in the Southcentral Pacific, and had taken part in many major engagements, but had seen few dead and no prisoners. As difficult as it had been in some respects, with the imminent threat from enemy submarines, from bombs and suicide planes, I had a bunk to sleep in and a meal, morning and evening. The street, and all of that it implied, was far off.

In late spring of that year I and a few of my fellow students decided that we would save our money and camp in tents on the dunes outside Provincetown where Hofmann's school was to move for the summer. For some reason, perhaps because I had by then some money saved in a small bank account, and because of my homesteading venture in Alaska I gave the impression of having had some needed experience, I found myself chosen to go out to the Cape early in order to sort out the situation and see what might be done, what we would need, and who we might turn to for help if we should need it.

Sometime in April, then, I took train and bus from New York to Provincetown. I made the serious mistake of not taking enough money with me, assuming I might go to a local bank and cash a check. When I arrived in Provincetown I found that I had spent nearly all my pocket money on bus and train fare. I went to a downtown bank, only to find that they would not accept my check, the lady behind the counter looking at me as if I were some kind of New York crook, or simply a drifter. I had not eaten that day since leaving New York, but was able to buy a cup of coffee at a cafe near the waterfront run by two Greek brothers, and to whom I explained my situation. Meanwhile, I had gone to the Chamber of Commerce at the town wharf, and had sent a wire to my bank; but I would have to wait until the following day for the money to arrive. Where was I to spend the night that was soon to come?

I went to a local roominghouse suggested to me by the cafe owners. I explained my problem to the landlady standing warily at the head of a steep stairway, and asked if I might have a room for the night; I would pay her the following day. No, she would not allow me a room. I then went to a nearby church and asked the priest for some help, a bed for the night. Again, I found no welcome. Night was coming on, it was chilly in the April dark. I returned to the cafe, where the Greek brothers gave me a meal, something to stay the hunger pangs. I was nearly twenty-six years old, already used to some hardships, but not until then had I faced a night on the street alone.

I walked Commercial Street, the main waterfront thoroughfare, searching and wondering. Finally I found an enclosed doorway in what appeared to be a vacant building. I had nothing with me but a light jacket and a small handbag, not having expected I might need bedding or a change of clothing. I curled up in the doorway out of sight of anyone walking the nearby street, and with my small bag for a pillow, managed a fitful, shivering slumber for some hours. It was then past midnight; I had stayed in the cafe until closing time, if only to keep warm. More than once during the night I got to my feet in the small rough space, moved my arms and legs to warm them, and lay down again in the dark. I could smell the wet salt air mixed with the sour dampness of the wood floor I was lying on; intermittently a fog horn pierced the darkness. Toward morning I became aware of the town fishermen on their way to the boats, their voices coming to me as if in sleep, their boots grating on the rough stone of the street. I slept again; it would be some time yet before the cafe opened.

And then day came. I had coffee and something to eat at the cafe close by, while I waited for my money to be wired from New York. And sometime later that morning it arrived. I paid the Greek brothers and thanked them for their kindness. And then, feeling that I had failed in what I had set out to do, I took bus and train back to Hartford and New York. I arrived late at the flat I shared on Stanton St. with my friend, Felix, and his wife; with some pained embarrassment I explained to them what had happened. It was a lesson, one I did not need to repeat.

After a summer spent tenting on the dunes with a small group of my fellow students, mostly afoot, walking the two or three miles into town (another but healthier version of the street), I rented a small cottage in Provincetown and devoted some quiet weeks to writing and walking the empty beaches. I returned to New York in November, and to our shared apartment. By then it had become obvious that the place was too small for the three of us, and I would have to find another space for myself.

Searching half-heartedly through the neighborhood, for the city was still scary and strange to me, I found a room in a run-down building a few blocks up Stanton Street, and moved in with my typewriter and the rest of my scarce belongings. I paid $20. a month for that room, hardly bigger than a closet. So far as I could tell, the building was occupied by impoverished immigrants, and I listened until late at night to the conversation in Spanish of a couple in the room next to mine.

I soon discovered that the room was infested with cockroaches, with bedbugs, fleas, and mice. I had not slept there long before I found myself itching and scratching, bitten from head to foot by the bugs I found impossible to rid myself of, and despite the insect powders and sprays I made use of—whatever was available at the time. I came to school one day, depressed, my face and neck spotted with red welts. A friend, the painter Franz Kline, stopped me on the stairway to the Hofmann studio and asked what had happened to me. I told him, and he said, in an urgent voice I can still recall: "John! Move out!" But it was not so easily done.

I spent no more time in that room than was necessary in order to sleep and be out of the weather. Between sessions at school I worked at my poems, using a chair as a prop for my typewriter, all the while watching for the bugs. Finally, however, after a few short weeks, I had to get out of it, as nothing seemed to relieve me of the pests in the bedding and woodwork. The enforced isolation had become oppressive, and my depression over it was increasing.

Three young women students at Hofmann's, whom I had met in Provincetown, rented a loft not far from the building where I was camping. Learning of my situation, they invited me to dinner one evening. I had by then decided to leave my infested room, but doing so threatened to put me on the street, as there was nowhere I could afford to move to. Later that evening, with a blanket and pillow loaned to me by friends, I went down to the

East River at the foot of Stanton Street, found a bench by the water, and resolved to spend the night.

I slept uneasily, awakened from time to time by a boat on the river, by traffic on the street above, by voices in the near distance. It was by then deep winter, and chilly on that open bench. Sometime after midnight I awoke to a light shining in my face. I sat up, alarmed, to find two police officers on patrol who had seen me there and stopped to ask if I was all right. A little shaken by the encounter, I explained my situation, told them that it was only temporary, that I did not intend to remain there. Satisfied that I was not ill or in danger, the officers wished me a good night, and left.

I went back to sleep. It is in some odd way a tribute to the state of things in those days that even in so rundown a part of New York I was in no apparent danger of being robbed or molested. Today it might have been a very different story.

The night passed. I awoke in the morning, gathered my blanket and pillow, and, stiff and sore from a night on that hard bench, I went to find some breakfast. Not long after that, my women friends, Jo, Louise, and Peggy, agreed that I could share their loft, which was large, and until I found something else. No more bugs, no more nights on the street or the threat of that. I had found a haven, and good company.

Early the following year, Peggy and I were married at the Manhattan Courthouse, and moved from Stanton Street to a small apartment near Third Avenue. There too we were reminded of the nearby lurking poverty: men sleeping in the doorway to our building, the never-ending coal soot on the windowsill, the occasional bug in our bedding, and like a deep underground menace, the shaking rumble of the elevated train night and day.

Years later I read George Orwell's <u>Down and Out in London and Paris</u>, and understood something of a kind of brotherhood among the less fortunate in our sometimes too comfortable world.

The street is still there, still home to the many thousands who do not share in our temporary wealth, ease and convenience. One may view these people as nuisance to be swept aside, or as a kind of conscience, half-visible but never entirely hidden–a haunting of a condition that may yet return.

As I write these words, I think of the Washington Metro stations, of the men (and sometimes women) camped there with their rough bags of clothing, their plastic cups held out for whatever one may think to give them. Of Pioneer Square in Seattle, in a district once known as Skid Road, and which remains so for many; of a bench in the park there, beneath which I once saw a pool of blood. I think too of a woman with two small children whom I discovered one evening sheltered in a corner doorway in downtown Washington, and to whom I spoke and offered help. Because of my early experience, brief though it was, I have never been able to walk away from these people without giving something, if no more than a dollar or two, a few coins. I understand, as the saying goes, that there, but for some saving grace, I might have been.

18 Aug 09

Dear Rachel,

    In one of your letters to me you mentioned your "Cats"! I don't know how many you have, but when I saw this card image I thought I would send it to you, and with good wishes. These two kitties look pretty happy together, though I thought at first they were curled up in a bowl of milk! Hmmm...maybe? I'm not a house-pet person, though I once kept a couple of cats for a friend, and one of them, the female, gave birth to a kitten one evening while sleeping in bed next to me, and I woke up with this little baby kitten next to my face, and the mother once more gone to sleep! Quite an event, and I had no idea it was on the way. I later gave the kitten away to a good home, or so I hoped it was.

    I miss hearing from you, Rachel, but I can guess you are pretty busy, and you have your house and mate to deal with, as well as your cats. But if I in any way have offended you, please do write and let me know. I owe you so much for your friendship and care at a time when it was needed, and I hope to see you once more down there, if not (maybe) here. Hard to say what I may be doing in the coming weeks and months, but there will be class to deal with, a book, and a good many other things, including my age and health, etc.

    I sent Kathy a note, thanking her for the Irish bottle, and also the wine. I hope things are going well down there.

    Love,
    John

[In John's handwriting:]
*Did you read my essay
"On The Street"? What did
you think of it?*

21 Aug 09

Dear Rachel,

I had just sent off to you my last letter, and the following day your card and 8 page letter was in the box! What a great surprise, and a gift also. No need for you to apologize for your handwriting; I had no trouble reading it, despite an occasional error or stumble. You write well, Rachel, and I think you should take it more seriously and make a decision as to what you might like to write about for possible publication. It is your thought, as well as the writing, that moves me to say this. So, please give it some thought; you have talent!

Among other minor errors, you mention having read Block. I assume you meant Broch, the Austrian/German novelist? [I mentioned French historian Marc Bloch, 1886-1944] Another question: you refer to Rosa Luxemburg and the film I told you of. But you refer to DVD, and to my knowledge the film is not available on DVD, only in the older format, VHS. But if you found a DVD copy of it, please let me know; I would love to get it, buy it, whatever. I like very much your thoughts as to a Rosa event, something calling attention to her life and efforts in support of a German republic, following on WW I. I'm with you on that. Did you find a copy of the film, watch it? I'd like to know about that.

I found it more than merely interesting what the History Prof. had to say in regard to Weimar. I think that a subject worthy of a history course there, and including the role of Rosa. There is plenty of material on this, and a good library search can reveal it. I don't know about the UAA library there, but the Rasmuson Library here has enormous stacks of older books on the upper floor of the library, and I have spent time there in the past. Sad to say, there is seldom a student to be found there; they don't read!

As for my poem, "Night", the question you asked about it: you will find in the "Notes" pages of my collected poems the essential story of that poem, how I came to write it, the various sources, etc. So, give it a look. You name the short poem, "Harvest" as one of your favorites. That poem is close to a translation of a poem by the German poet, Hölderlin. [Friedrich Hölderlin, German poet and philosopher, 1770-1843.] This is also among the "Notes" section.

You have introduced so much in your 8 pages plus, and it is getting late for me, my often tired eyes at this time of the evening. I will add to this letter tomorrow. Meanwhile, much to think about, and my thanks to you for all that you've had to say, and ask!

Love,
John
 [arrow to next page]

Sat., 8/22

Before mailing this to you, I thought to include one or two more items that you might find worth reading and thinking about... The page I enclose is one I found especially interesting, and mainly due to the brief comment on Sophie Scholl, her brother and companion. I may have mentioned this before: the movie I found in a video store here, and having watched it I bought a copy of it. Not a Hollywood star performance, etc., but essentially a documentary, and the column on the page tells the story. The film is not hard to find, and I have seen it on Blockbuster shelves here in town, as well as in another video store. If you have not seen it, I think you should, and I think you will be as impressed by it as I was and still am. Another page in our modern history, one that we all need to turn and think about. The other stories on this page are equally important: persons and events most of us know nothing of. My own feeling for our common humanity is in many ways enriched by my discovery of these events and individuals: how a girl or neighbor down the street might act in so heroic a way and make a major difference in the lives of others.

So, more to think about and write about. Your mention of possibly coming up here with Kathy for a visit is a welcome idea, and let me know when and if you decide to do it. I am also interested in your family background, where you came from, where you have lived, and so forth. You told me you were born in San Diego, but also mentioned having lived in New York. And in your letter I note time spent in Santa Cruz, and how many other places? I had assumed you were basically a New York Jew who somehow had gone astray and ended up in Alaska, the Far North! Well, I ended up here also, after life lived in many different places.

Rachel, I will put an end to this, and send it off to you as soon as I can. If I can think of anything else to write or send you, I'll do so. Meanwhile, I give you a distant hug and thank you for all that you had to tell me. I feel energized by this, and that is good for an elder like me!

Love,
John

8/23/09

Sunday:

Rachel, a couple of notes that might interest you:

Your list of my poems includes "Rain Country," one of my own favorites from that period. I wrote the poem while living in a house on the peninsula west of Seattle during the fall and winter of 1978-79. The rain season came on, and as I looked out at the leaves on the maples and other trees I was acutely reminded of the fall up North and my old homestead. I began writing the poem then, but it required a few more years for me to finish it, and after my return to Fairbanks and Richardson in 1980.

The brief poem that precedes "Rain Country," "Tenderfoot," was written earlier and then revised during the time I finished "Rain Country." It is one of my poems I can recite to myself and often do. I can still see young Jessie standing at the door of the cabin she shared with her father as I was about to leave, having spent a day and night there, helping her father, Emery, spade and plant their summer garden. Jessie was 17, an Athabaskan girl, who died two years later, age 19, smitten with her TB. A few old logs of their cabin by the roadside are still there, as I recall from a brief look a few years ago. Sad story, I guess, but I'm glad I was able to write the poem in remembrance.

John

27 Aug 09

Dear Rachela,

Another nice card and good letter from you. You ask: do I prefer short or longer letters? Well, it depends on who is writing and what they have to say! But yours are always welcome, short or longer, cards or letter pages.

You apparently had not received the long letter-card I sent not long after getting yours. Our letters do cross, it seems, but I will try to keep that in mind and not get things too confused between us.

. . cats? Dear God, I'd run for a shelter somewhere. Maybe I should address you as "Scratchy"? Or maybe: "Scratchel"? Well, you and your partner seem able to cope with that, but I couldn't, no Ma'm —or Mom!

At some point not long ago I think you asked me if I had some new work, poems or prose, that I might send you a copy of. I enclose here two fairly recent poems which you might find worth reading and/or thinking about. "The Elder Birch" is a rewrite of the closing verse in my long sequence, "Forest Without Leaves." For reasons that remain obscure, I was moved to adapt the poem to my present time of increasing age, while keeping intact the general form of it and the words I used in sequence, etc. I think it works pretty well, and it was published last year in a journal edited by a former UAF student, Robert Hedin, who very much liked it. [*Great River Review*, issue 48, 2008] Great River Review is based in Minnesota where Hedin has lived since graduating from UAF in the 1970s.

The other poem is one of a number I wrote in the late 1990s, influenced by the Roman poet, Horace, whose direct address of friends and others for whom he is writing, caught my attention, and I wrote several poems under that influence. "For the Century's End" may not have been published, but I remain uncertain about that. The others have been, in one journal or another.

So, read and think, and let me know what you think. If I have at hand here another something more recent, I'll send a copy of it when the time feels right for it.

So, I'll close this off. I had a lot to say in my last, longer, letter, but don't let the length of things worry you. You say I am "never far from your heart." Well, you are always <u>in</u> my heart, and I will never let you escape, or use one of your older cats to hide you!

Love,
John

(I might have more to say, but I need to get out to the PO and buy some stamps. My letter-writing consumes them by the hour and the day!)

John Haines
20 Nielson Ln
Lenox, MA 01240

THE ELDER BIRCH

In a forest without leaves
I stand, slender and white.

Though the sun drank color
from my leaves, and the marrow
in my roots froze down,

more than my paper bark
remains to weather and peel—
let the wind take away all the rest.

Whenever you come again, you will
know this tree. More than a leaf
held fast in darkness,

I still quietly burn,
and I'll give you some light.

2007
John Haines

TO THE CENTURY'S END
after Horace

Shorten sail, no matter the wind:
master of the wild hills no longer,
each day may be the last,
and we are but dust and shadow.

When the preacher mounts the pulpit
the poet flees, resigns his office.
But if the poet fails to speak,
becomes a tenured puppet—what then?

Think, in this haunted, congested age,
how few acres are left for the plow
by the great sprawl of housing,
and how the corporate temples tower.

Then make the buildings taller, for when
they fall we'll not fail to hear them.
Long in the empire's aftermath
they too will be dust and shadow.

It is the century's end. No Caesar
for us, not yet, only the bickering
public men—an idle circus,
the state come to a thrifty standstill.

I think of my house in a far woodland,
the gate locked, the mailbox fallen;
of a country school, its classroom silent,
closed now to all but the darkness.

No moon, and the wine bottle empty.
On the stripped hills and vacant fields
a cold wind scatters the leaves.

1999

02 Sept 09

Dear Rachel,

My DC friend, Miles Moore, told me in a recent note that the Haines Group would be meeting there on Aug 27, and he would talk with them about your suggestion, and would let you know of the result…

Love,
John

---

7 Sept 09

Dear Rachel,

Thank you for this 4-page recent letter, so filled with so much, and I had no trouble reading it. I was pleased to read of your many places where you lived as a younger person, and I was also glad to read of your family story: old folks from the Old Country, and so forth. You asked if I ever met an Elkenbaum? I never saw or heard the name before.

Among the many places you have lived, you mention [near] Paterson, NJ. You may know of WC Williams' long poem by that name, though he himself lived in another small town as a family doctor. I guess it wasn't far from Paterson. But then we come to all these places from coast to coast: Santa Cruz, Venice, New York, Long Island, Hoboken, Seattle, and then Anchorage, etc. Why don't you move up here, to Delta or North Pole, with all your cats? Or Bethel, Circle City, etc...? Might as well do it all, Lady Epstein!

As for applying for some money for a possible biography project, why not go ahead and do it? You may have access to the needed details, etc., and more so than I have at this time. I can always confirm that you do so with my approval. Just what this might mean, or involve, I am uncertain, but I'll certainly give it my support, and whatever might be needed in background information, etc. Thank you for making the suggestion. I am at this time very involved with preparing for this semester class, and I have no time or energy for anything at this moment. Not a lot of time ahead, but I'll leave it to you to do whatever is needed. Thanks for asking and suggesting.

As for my poem, "Night", and so many others, of course the background, or source for that poem goes much farther back than the photos and pictures I have seen of great paintings and sculptures. The poem, or poems, are founded on the life I lived, mainly in Interior Alaska, with all that was available to me in the landscape, the seasons, the dark and the light, the borealis, the life that was and is there and which I came to know, not as scientific observer but as one who lived the life that was there to be lived, and the obvious necessity of it. The art work I came to know much later and which returned me to the time I spent in the study of art in the big city schools I went to, simply, or not so simply, an instinctive reconciliation. But what I am saying here is not an adequate response to what you ask, or say, in regard to the poem. It is dense, packed with details, references, etc. ... Little wonder that many readers may never fully understand it. But the underlying music of the verse conveys to an alert ear the essential substance of it. At least it does to my ear, simply as a reader.

But returning to Alaska, the background of my writing, this past weekend I spent some time with a friend in Denali, and we drove the

Denali Highway east toward Paxon and as far as Maclaren Summit, one of the places I have seen and absorbed as part of myself, and have at one time or another referred to in a poem or some prose. We had a lovely two days down there, the weather perfect.

So, now I must get back to the coming classwork I need to clarify for the students who will be there on Wednesday. It won't be easy, but I'll do my best with it, and probably for the last time.

Love,
John

Thanks again for the letter, always good to read and think about!

13 Sept 09

Dear Rachel,

Well, it looks as if your last card and note were sent to me before you got my last long letter. As has been the case, our letter/cards have crossed, but I hope my last one engages your thoughts, and I'll look for a response whenever you want to write to me again. No hurry about that.

As for Boraas' [Alan Boraas (1947-2019), former professor of Anthropology at Kenai Peninsula College, UAA] column and the Native land situation, I cannot recall during the statehood arguments and events any reference to Native Alaskans and their lack of a substantial role at the time. Those few I met with at the time, mainly locals along the highway and in the region, were mainly concerned about the consequences of statehood, and many of us were not in favor of it. During the '60s there was one infamous event involving then-Senator Gruening and the Rampart Dam proposal for the lower Yukon River. I won't attempt to tell the whole story here, but it would have had a terrible effect on Native villages and their ways of life. I wrote a letter to the local paper at the time, in support of the Native people and their situation in direct opposite to what the Senator was telling people. The paper printed my letter, and I think the Senator wrote something in defense of his proposal, etc. I can't give details here, but it was a more than merely interesting episode. It was a major interest also that had the dam project succeeded, it would have been named: Gruening Dam! Well, I'm glad we were able to defeat it. Politicians, no matter their seniority, never give up…Rats, vermin, or merely rascals! There are a lot of events, issues, and stories, that many folks today know little or nothing about, and it's good that Boraas… brought this up.

…So, that's it for the moment. As for life at Richardson, and politics, there was no immediate effect on us there during that time. We read or heard about things, but played no part in any of it…

Love,

John

As for the "Group" problem, I'm sure you will hear from good friend Miles when the time comes. He is a good man, and if he makes a promise he will keep it.

[ENCLOSED NOTECARD]
Madison Park Greetings, Inc.

"HOW BEAUTIFUL A DAY CAN BE
WHEN KINDNESS TOUCHES IT."
   George Ellistan

THANK YOU

[In John's handwriting:]

*Yes, and thank you
too for remembering
me!
 Love,
 John*

2 Oct 09

Dear Rachel,

    Thank you for the card and letter, as always. I love getting the news, etc., that you have to send me, even if it is a bit disappointing. I appreciate your looking into the possibility of a grant from AHF [Alaska Humanities Forum]; I am not familiar with that organization, but it would have been great had your effort succeeded. As for the other sources, you might look into a Rasmuson possibility. They have the money, but of course have made it possible for me to be awarded by the USA [Artists] organization. I'm sure there are other sources for a grant or something for this elder poet. I don't know anyone at the NEA in Washington, but the former chair, Dana Gioia, has been a good friend, and he might have been able, and willing, to be of some help. I don't know what else to suggest.

    I'm very glad to hear of the Rosa group at UAA, and I am glad I introduced you to Rosa, her life and time. When you know more about the event, time and place, let me know; I might just make it down there for it. If I can think of [anyone] here at UAF who might also take some interest in this, I'll mention it to him or her, or them, and let you know. This sort of thing is very much what we are in need of at this time. Which reminds me that I found a paperback copy of <u>Suite Francaise</u> in a bookstore back east a couple of years ago, and I bought it to send to a friend I thought might like to read it. I'm glad someone there is making some use of it for a class...

... Yes, I reread my stories and essays, and especially when I have a class to deal with. I have recently introduced my small group of young women to several of my pieces, including one or two so far uncollected, and it seems to work pretty well in stirring their interest in writing.

I have also given them copies of articles and stories I've read and copied from some of the journals and papers I read, subscribe to, etc. I like doing this sort of thing, and it seems to work very well, and also stimulates my own creative energies, even when we may disagree about some issue, opinion, or whatever.

So, many thanks for your good words, your interest and concerns, I did, by the way, get a flu shot, and I have read recently that a Swine Flu shot will be available here in a week or so. I was ill for a couple of days last week, and could not explain or guess what caused it. But I spoke with my health care person today, and she told me that what I described to her about my brief affliction sounded like the Swine flu. So, when the medicine arrives, I am to be sure and get the shot, just to be certain.

When I have some date for coming down there, I'll let you know. I owe Kathy a letter also, and have been rather overwhelmed with stuff lately, including my new book [*Descent*] and various details needed clarification, correcting, etc. But I always look forward to your letters, so write again or whenever you have something to tell me, ask about, or send me...

Love,
John

29 Oct 09

Dear Rachel,

So good to have your card and letter. I had not heard from you for some time, and of course assumed you were down south in California with family and had no time to write to folks up here in the frigid North!

But I very much appreciated the bookstore news, and your words on me and my work... Perhaps it is appropriate that after so long a life devoted to Letters there appears to be some new recognition of that old faker, Haines. You know he never lived the life he's written about so much; he just made it all up, driving a cab in New York the whole time!

Thanks for letting me know about the Rosa Luxemburg event; if I can make it, I'd like to be there for it. Will the film be shown? I hope so. Pretty amazing that a figure like Rosa whom not many know of, would attract an event like this.

You ask if my work has been translated. There are poems in Spanish, I believe, and in German also. A major fact is that my memoir, <u>The Stars, The Snow, The Fire,</u> was published in a French edition in 2005. I had no idea this was in progress, and then the publisher, Editions Gallmeister, sent me a copy, and told me that it was being read over there. I can't read French, but it was an impressive thing to hold in hand and look at it. If I still have copy to spare, I'll send it to you.

Some wet sticky snow here, a mess to drive in; but it has turned colder and the mush has frozen. Almost November, and a long warm fall until now. I miss the mild days, but I'll do my best to stay warm, or wait until you come...

Thanks for writing. I hope your...cats are warm.

Love,
John

PS: Why can't these socalled Haines enthusiasts work to provide the old fellow with some financial security in his elder years? A pension, some retirement fund?

ॐ

15 Nov 09

Dear Rachel,

Thank you for your letter and card which I received a couple of days ago. I'm sorry you have lost a cat, but how many can you expect to keep and for how long?

You ask about the new book [*Descent*], and I have enclosed a slip with the needed information. I don't know the price of it, but I'm sure you can get the needed info from Florenz [at CavanKerry Press] or whoever opens the mail back there. She is the managing editor. Copies won't be available until sometime in March. I suspect. But thanks for your interest in it, and maybe adding a few copies to your bookstore!

As for the Rosa event, thanks for letting me know I will have a place to stay, and with thanks to Kathy. I can't be certain that I'll be able to make it, but will keep it in mind for March 1. There is a flight cost I have to deal with, and if I am to teach a spring class I need to check on the dates. I am not certain I have anything to add to a discussion on Rosa and her life and work, other than my admiration for her and the life she gave to that period in German History. I've tried to arouse some interest in having the film on her life issued in the DVD form, but so far nothing has come of that. It deserves a serious attention from scholars and students, etc.

An old friend, one of the Haines Group, Marcella Wolfe, was here for a brief visit. She stayed with another friend, but we met a couple of times and had a lot of good talk. She lives and works in Wash DC, but also has a place out in West Virginia. It is always good to see her and discuss so much that we share. Were it possible, I'm sure she'd love to be there for the Rosa meeting.

As for me, I'm still here and still on my feets. I'm having trouble with my vision, mainly my right eye, and will have a visit at the Eye Clinic here tomorrow. I can't read well if the print is small, and I make use of a magnifying glass often.

As for my class, things are going well. The young gals are good writers, and they also <u>think</u>, even when they do not always agree with my view of things, like current poetry, and/or current politics, the state the nation, our land and the effects of corporate dominance, etc. I have perhaps four more class meetings before the semester ends. I am very pleased, happy to have met with these young people, and I wish them well with their studies, wherever that will take them.

Thanks for making it possible for the bookstore to have a few copies of my chapbook [*Of Your Passage, O Summer*, Limberlost Press] from the press in Boise, Idaho, and it is always good to hear that the CD is selling.

I can't recall if I mentioned the Fall issue of <u>Sewanee Review</u>, which has a surprising and very important essay on my first book, <u>Winter News</u>, by the writer, Marc Hudson. I think you and others would find it worth reading, and the magazine isn't hard to find, or order. ["A Voice at Once Contemporary and Ancient, the Enduring Value of John Haines's *Winter News*," Sewanee Review, Volume 117, Number 4, Fall 2009] ...

...Thank you again, and always, for writing. You can give Buster my wishes for his good health. I also get a periodic steroid treatment for my lower back, and it works! It doesn't last, but I get it every two months, and am due for another next month. Age is a pain, Buster [the cat on the card]...

Love,
John ...

[In John's handwriting:]

*Cold here, but not much
Snow. Subzero-yuk!*

[Typed] Book Title: DESCENT
                Due March 2010
    Florenz Eisman
    CavenKerry Press, Ltd.
    6 Horizon Rd., #2901
    Fort Lee, NJ 07024

ঌ

28 Nov 09

Dear Rachel,

It was good, as always, to have your card and brief letter. But the check you enclosed was an amazing thing, and I hardly know how to thank you for it. [The $700 gift was possible due to the 2009 Alaska Permanent Fund Dividend disbursement.] It was, is, something I would never have expected. Thank you for it, for thinking of me. I deposited it a couple of days ago, and there it is, to be used as needed…

…Yes, the publisher wrote me that my book [*Descent*] may be available early next year, and we will not wait until March. That's good news, and I hope it all works out for the best. But I will stay in touch, and let you know how things go.

Thanks again for your generosity.

    Love,
    John

11 Dec 09

Dear Rachel,

Thank you so much for sending me Marc Hudson's address, and for the copies of your email exchange. I have just written Marc, and will expect to hear from him soon. You are so good a friend, Rachel, and what would I do without you? Hmmmm...

I have had my last semester class, and all I need do now is hand in grades. It was as fine a group of students as I can recall having anywhere, at any time. All young women, and a very intelligent four. I will miss them, and I know they will remember me and all that I gave them to read and respond to. Whether I'll be able to teach another next year, remains a question. Age, for me, is a factor, and increasingly so. I hope to get my eyes in better shape for reading, and also, maybe, improving my hearing. The class missed having good class discussions due to my not being able to hear them well enough. But things went well in spite of this.

So, I will be waiting [for] copies of the new book, and meanwhile taking care of a lot of postponed stuff here: papers to sort and box, and perhaps work on a new memoir piece. Whether I'll come up with some new poems, hard to say, but maybe.

I have no plans for the holiday, but perhaps a meeting with a friend or two here, and the cooking of another roadkill special! Stuffed Porky, Braised Muskrat, Gluey Gopher, etc. And of course, the standard Moose-drop Stew! You'd love it all, I'm sure.

I had a good letter from Kathy Tarr and if all goes well I will look forward to meeting with all of you in March, if not before. I shall bring dear old Rosa with me, and you can bet on that. Which reminds me that there is a great older film now available on DVD: Dersu Uzala, Russian, dating from the early 1980s. If you ain't seen it, go look! I watched the other night, and was once more deeply moved.

I may have more to say or write later, but want to get this into the mail today. I am due for a Swine Flu shot this afternoon, and don't want to miss that. Too many Swine on campus, and you gotta watch it, you know!

Thank you again, dear Rachel...

Love,
John

---

21 Dec 09

Dear Rachel,

Thanks once more for your card and note, always for me a treasure to have and read.

Having finished up all the semester class papers, I am catching up on a lot of delayed correspondence, friends to whom I have owed a letter or card for some time. Everything seems to have slowed down for me these days, and do my best to get myself moving once more. I miss the girls in my class, and I hope to hear from one or two of them when school starts up again. But I have no plans for the spring semester. The book is due, though nothing certain as to when, and I have a lot of uncompleted work I need to get back to. The subzero temps have slowed me down, and I was glad to get out today and find it a good deal warmer. This old guy can't take it as he once did.

One thing we might attempt in regard to Rosa, and that is to get that film on her life and fate onto DVD. It can be done, I'm sure, and just needs a bit of urging among scholars and film-makers, etc.

I'll look forward to hearing from you again. Don't mind the overstuffed kitty: it's only me asleep on the couch!

Love,
John

[In John's handwriting:]
A photo of me on the porch
of a friend's house last fall—
a nice surprise to see the
old fellow with a drink, the
leaves still green in the background!

Photo enclosed.

On a Friend's Porch, Fall 2008

Correspondence 2010

[ENCLOSED NOTECARD]

MADISON PARK GREETINGS, INC.

"SANTA CLAUS HAS THE RIGHT IDEA.
VISIT PEOPLE ONCE A YEAR."

    Victor Borge

[January no date]

Rachel, I have a small request. I often fix some Indian food for my supper, and which I like much of the time. However, I would like to have some Indian bread to go with it. There is no Indian place here in Fairbanks, though there once was as I remember it back in the 1980s. But I recall the place we went to last year when I was down in Anchorage, and I wonder if you might stop by there and get me some of their bread. It has a name, but I can't remember it. It is, mostly, flat and dry, not like a loaf of anything, and should be easy to mail to me up here. I'll be more than glad to pay you any expense for this. So, when you get a chance, take a look down there at whatever the name was of the place where we ate so good a meal. I thank you in advance!

    John

7 Jan 10

Dear Rachel,

Once more, thank you for the card and all the news you had to give me. I was a bit surprised to learn that you saw "Dersu Uzala" in a New York theater; that must have been quite an event back then. I first saw the film at a theater here in Fairbanks in the 1980s, and I think I rented and watched it at least once at a later time. But I am reminded to mention another film you may or may not know of "The Third Man," which dates from 1948. I first saw it in a small theater in Washington, DC when I was then an art student at American University. I knew nothing about the movie, but it looked to me worth seeing, and I bought a ticket and went to see it. If you don't know about, it takes place in Vienna after WW II when the city was occupied by allied forces: British, American, Russian, etc., and the film starred a number of actors famous at the time, including Orson Wells. As a recent war vet I was immediately taken up with the film and its story, though I had not read the novel by Graham Greene on which it is based.

Well, not long ago, and to my surprise, I saw a DVD of the film in the local Blockbuster, and I immediately rented it, have watched it now three times! If you don't know it, I suggest you look for it and sit down and watch it! If you do, or have, I'd like to know about it and what you think.

Your story of the piece of land you once bought and planned [to] make into a home place, in some ways sounds all too familiar. It happens all too many times in these "progressive" times. I would like to have seen it if you were living there.

Things have not been easy for me of late, with the old back pain back again, and little relief from the prescriptions I continue to make use of. And my eyes continue to trouble me, with no real solution available so far. But I read, and with my sturdy magnifier in hand. What next? I ask of the doctor ghost who stands in the doorway or sits beside me. No answer.

I have finished reading through a copy of the new book [*Descent*] sent to me by the press back east, and I found a number of printing errors which I have passed on to the editor for correction. If all goes well (or ill!), we should see copies of it late this month or early next. I'll be sure to let you know, and if I have a copy to spare, I will send you one.

I'm glad I sent you a copy of that photo, and glad to hear that you liked it. The trees in that picture are very much like those at the old homestead in early fall, and I am reminded all too well just how things were back then when I was able to live there, keep the place in order, and once more be "at home." Here, I'm just a renter and a sitter! If I can find the right one, I will send on a copy of one of the older homestead photos for you.

So, the time gets on, and my visit to the bookstore event in March is closer. When the time comes, you can let me know any details of the visit I may need to know. At least by then the days will be longer, and possibly cooler! It is a bit milder here at the moment, but soon enough, "down she goes!"

I have a lot to do in the weeks ahead: sorting of papers, clearing out the many monthly or weekly periodicals I have piled here, and maybe putting together a suitable collection of my correspondence and class papers, etc., and which I can, I hope, send off to the library at Ohio U., which now has a very large collection of my stuff. I would hate having to toss it all out, But I don't need to.

So, stay in touch, and I always love getting your cards and writing. Thank you for it, and I hope your cat colony is well!

Love,
John

17 Jan 10

Dear Rachel,

Once more, thank you for your incredible generosity in sending me all the India goods; I did not expect anything like it. The package arrived yesterday in good time and condition.

And for the copy of the <u>Northern Review.</u> Ross Coen had given me a copy when it came out, but I may not have mentioned that to you in one of my recent letters. I had previously read a copy of his piece which he had given me to read and check for errors, etc. It was too late to correct a few things, but if he should decide to include the story in some future collection, he should have a few stray facts corrected. If I did not mention this, a major error occurs in his first paragraph: that is, it was not Peg who was with me on that visit to old Fred's Lake Camp after he died, but my second wife and longtime companion, Jo, who was with me; a major hike for her, being new in the country and not familiar with old Fred.

As for the Rosa event, I am not certain what I might have to say about her, with all the scholars you have enlisted for the meeting; but I will give this some thought, and hopefully be ready when the time comes. I may be able to write a poem for it, but nothing certain. I'm glad you are promoting the possibility of the film on her life and fate in a new DVD edition. It can be done, and all it takes is for the makers to decide to do it! I will mention this to the director of the library here at UAF. It was she who got the Russian film, "Burnt By the Sun," issued in DVD form, following on my having asked for it more than once. So, we'll see what comes of it.

As for my papers, etc., you have misread what I told you of this: they are not with the library at Cincinnati, but with the Alden Library at Ohio University—a very different place. I was able to give my papers to them because of the time I spent teaching there in 1989-90. It would never have occurred to me to approach anyone at Cincinnati.

Thank you also for suggesting the prospect of future academics studying the Haines legacy. Well, maybe, and I think it will happen, and perhaps my independence in the academic market will help correct some of our present emphasis on a "career," as if a true poet could not exist without an MFA! As I sometimes ask: what sort of MFA did Keats have? [John Keats (1795-1821) English Romantic Poet], or Rainer Rilke? [Rainer Maria Rilke (1875-1926), Austrian poet and novelist.]

Incidentally, when I first looked over your card, I thought you had written "Bill Moyers" as one of the Rosa speakers! And then, of course, I saw that it was "Meyers"!

It is always an event for me to receive another letter from you, Rachel; few folks these days write so well and often.

It has warmed a bit today, and I'm damned glad of that. This long stretch of subzero has sapped my energies, and it has not been easy for me to get moving in the morning, return to some of the writing I need to do, while coping also with my troubled eyesight. But I'm still here, and will look for another card/letter from you whenever you have something to tell me!

Thanks to Kathy also, and I will make plans for the trip to Anchorage when the time comes.

Love,
John

PS: We are to meet on March 1, which is a Monday. Would it be best for me to come down earlier that day, or on Sunday afternoon? You say I am due for two nights at Kathy's, which would include Sunday and Monday evenings. Right? There is plenty of time to make my flight plans, but I thought to ask about it, just in case, etc. I hope you can meet me at the airport! If not, I may cancel out.

5 Feb 10

Dear Rachel,

As always, thank you for the card and letter; no matter how brief, it is always worth waiting for and reading.

I spoke with a travel agent today, and have made plans for the flight to Anchorage. I am to leave here at 4pm on Sunday, and due to arrive about 5pm. My return flight on Tuesday will leave at 10am. I will have more specific details, flight numbers, etc., when I pick up the ticket on Monday. It ain't cheap, well over $200., and were it not for the generous check you sent me a while ago, I might have to cancel out of this event. My finances, expenses, are getting more difficult to maintain. But I look forward to seeing you again and spending some time together, and with Kathy and others. I'm not certain what I might say about Rosa, but I'm sure others there will make it all worthwhile.

Yes, we can discuss my work before we check in with Rosa; I leave that up to you. Just don't try to record it, and then put it up for sale!

Well, I'm feeling the cold and the years more and more, and ere the daytime is over I am ready for bed and another long sleep.

Incidentally, I rented not long ago a film I had not heard of before, another look at WW II and the German side of it: DRESDEN, mainly documentary but with a number of men and women who act the parts you would expect to see. It came in two parts, and I watched them both in two nights. Pretty grim, if you know the story, the devastation of the city from the British bombing, and close to the end of the war.

My DESCENT is due pretty soon, maybe next week, according to what a friend learned from Amazon. So, we'll see, and if I get a few advanced copies I'll let you know.

So, enough for the time being. I always look for your cards and letters, and I am more than grateful for them.

Love,
John

19 Feb 10

Dear Rachel,

Here is a copy of my flight schedule, and I hope it remains accurate as to times of departure and arrival. I will check on this next week, just to be sure.

Thank you once more for the card and your more than friendly words. I can appreciate that my work as writer, as poet, is in certain respects unique, unlike any of my contemporaries. You ask where are the poets today? Well, they are all, with an exception here and there like Wendell Berry, [American/Kentuckian poet, farmer, novelist, environmental critic, born in 1934] locked up in their tenured slots and with little or no reason to speak up on social and political issues, and especially if they are still in search of permanence in an academic position. The MFA system has simply cancelled for most university poets any possibility of being heard in response to any serious subjects or issues "outside the box." As a few individuals here and there have said or written on occasion, if you want to keep your job or tenure, just keep your mouth shut and teach another literature class or writing workshop!

Well, from the beginning I've been more or less an outsider, though there are, have been, many former students and colleagues who might testify to my excellence as a teacher, and more than one person has written in response to this. But I'm sure you know about it, and I needn't say more.

The artwork on the card you sent, by a Tibetan refugee child, is more than striking... pretty amazing, compared to what you might get from an American school kid.

I'm reading Rosa's letters and the biographical background, and learning a lot—more than I thought I knew of her life and social-political activity. A rare woman, I think. Whether I'll have anything to say worth a bit of time in this event, I'm not certain. But we can talk about this and that in the Tea cup discussion, whatever seems right to you ... I look forward to seeing you again!

 Love,
 John

PS: I think the 1pm option might be the best for me, but whatever works for you will be okay.

5 March 10

Dear Rachel,

 I think I mentioned to you while I was still in Anchorage, the letter I am sending a copy of which was published in the <u>Fairbanks Daily News-Miner</u> shortly after I sent it as a letter to the editor. I had sent a copy previously to the <u>Seattle Times</u>, but never had a response, and it was a rewarding surprise to find it on the editorial page of a Sunday edition here in Fairbanks.

 I will enclose also another letter I wrote in response to a brief piece I saw in the <u>Atlantic Monthly</u> sometime after I had written my letter on the 9/11 events. Nothing came of this, no reply from the editor, but I still feel that it speaks the truth in regard to American dominance of smaller Latin countries like Cuba. Perhaps things are changing a bit with the relative retirement of Fidel Castro, but we can never be certain, given another major shift in American policies, the possible election of another Republican president, etc.

 Anyway, I thought these two letters from the Alaska laureate might engage your interest, whether or not you agree with all that I have to say.

And once more, Rachel, I want to thank you for your presence there in Anchorage this past week, always ready to be of help to me, and keenly alert to whatever is going on. I owe you, and Kathy, a big thanks for hosting me, arranging the meetings I took part in, and much else. My good friend, John Kooistra, was waiting for me at the terminal here when I arrived, and I was able to return to the house here, unpack, and relax. It doesn't take much to tire me these late days and years, but I had a good sleep and have been able to take care of a number of things that were needed.

I rented, by the way, from the university library a copy of the Rosa L. film, still in the VHS form, but I have mentioned to the lady at the desk that we need to have it available in the DVD form, and I hope that happens.

I send my best to you always, and my enduring gratitude for your friendship, your help when needed!

Love,
John

(Rachel, if you can find the best means to send it to me, I would like to have a copy of the large poster for our Rosa project. I could not fit it in with my briefcase, etc.; if I can get one I will get it framed and have it on the wall here!)

[arrow to next page]

PS: I got a copy of the Rosa film from UAF library here, and hope to watch it soon. In older tape edition, of course, but I will persist in trying to get it available in the DVD mode. It very much deserves this, as you know and agree with. Let us fight for it! No surrender, please!

MAY THE OWL CALL AGAIN

John Haines
622 Ridgecrest Dr.
Fairbanks, 99709
479-0509

30 Aug 02

Letters to the Editor
Fairbanks Daily News-Miner
PO Box 70710
Fairbanks 99707

WHY?: One Answer To the Question

On considering the present and growing conflict in which this nation is now engaged—the "war on terrorism," the global economic, political, and ethnic forces involved—it has appeared to me that in certain important respects we have entered on a religious war. I do not mean by this a struggle between traditional faiths, between Jews, Muslims and Christians, but something more complex and encompassing, and in part suggested to me several years ago by a comment in the writings of Noam Chomsky: that for America and the West, but especially for America, capitalism has become the state religion, its priesthood anointed by a corporate wealth and overwhelming influence, and by government complicity. I have thought of this often, and especially following on the events of September 11: the militant fervor in the killing of people representative of an opposing belief, one that appears to have taken over much of the modern world, having bestowed on "free trade," as the writer Wendell Berry has phrased it, "the status of a god."

My sense of this has been further informed by images of the New York City skyline and the towering structures that have until recently symbolized for us the ruling powers. While sitting at a sidewalk table in downtown Seattle last year, in an area dominated by nearby office complexes, I looked down 4th Avenue toward an older building, a church or a mosque, a graceful structure from the past, once prominent in the early years of the city. The impression has remained with me, a symbol of our modern predicament: that what was once a common faith represented by the cathedral and the neighborhood church, is now overshadowed by the corporate towers where in fact our true faith would seem to lie, promoted and celebrated in the pages of our major newspapers and journals as "the cathedral of commerce."

I do not condone the drastic events of September 11, but I believe that a certain justice can be acknowledged in having the tallest, most prominent symbols of a secular faith based on consumerism, on trade and profit, attacked and destroyed by extremists of a much older religion. I remain convinced that had we, during the Muslim Ramadan month earlier this year, halted our bombing of Afghanistan and made clear that we did so out of respect for Islamic religion, we might have accomplished far more in gaining respect and support among the Arabic nations.

Related to what I have written here, and especially in reference to the causalities of 9/11, is our misuse of the word "innocent." If you accept a position with a global corporation, an office in a prominent edifice like the New York trade towers, with all the social and monetary advantages these imply, you are not innocent; you have become a part of the problem, a willing accomplice, operative in all that it represents; the imposition of a global economic system on traditional ways of life, the dislocation and impoverishment of rural peoples. The true innocents are the displaced residents of exploited lands, the women and children among the refugees in Afghanistan and elsewhere; not the corporate executives and their staffs, nor the officials who support them and their practice.

All if this may be argued, amplified and corrected, but it cannot be ignored. We may have entered a new, perhaps final, phase of human existence that will be resolved only by a deeper understanding than is currently evident; and beyond that a measure of forgiveness not now visible. The choice otherwise can only be a mutual annihilation, the destruction of civilization as we have known it. The global triumph of American capitalism can be temporary at best, and will only hasten an age of deterioration and a final defeat of those human virtues we cherish. Our present administration appears to be a very long way from that required understanding.

ಎ

10 Sept 04

Letters to the Editor
The Atlantic Monthly
77 North Washington St.
Boston, MA 02114

Dear Editor:

The brief comment on Cuba in your October issue (p. 62) serves once more to reflect the longstanding conflict between that small island nation and the United States. We continue to treat Cuba as if it were an American colony, which in many respects it has been for all too long a time. Rather than discuss abstractly the possibility of a major change in the relationship if and when Castro leaves the scene, we need to enact at least two major changes in policy. One: end the trade embargo and all related impositions on an independent country; two: ease all travel restrictions to and from Cuba for Americans and other citizens of the world.

It is time also that we returned to Cuba the Guantanamo Bay military base, and in doing so opened the possibility of a useful dialogue with Castro and other members of the Cuban community. We should cease to treat that country as if it were a breakaway American property and subject to our laws and corporate interests. It is their land, has always been, and we have no moral right to occupy even a small part of it for our own purposes.

Whatever the flaws in Castro's governance of his country, we are not politically or morally appointed to judge this small island nation and its people. If there is to be a long overdue revision in our attitude and approach to Cuba, whether during the present Bush term of office, or in a new democratic administration, the time is now.

Sincerely,
John Haines
John Haines

॰॰

18 March 10

Dear Rachel,

Thank you as always for your good letter. Apparently you had not received the card I sent you after the wonderful arrival of the Rosa posters. If you still haven't got it, let me know. I was so taken with the sight of those wonderful color designs, the face of Rosa, and so much else. I have yet to find the right place and person to have at least one of the posters mounted, or framed, so that I can post it on the wall here, but it will happen. Once, as a visual artist, I might have done it myself, but haven't the means at hand here. But thank you once more, Rachel, for responding so quickly to my request. I did not expect more than one of the posters, but there were three in the tube, another fact to your credit.

As for your question, re my "companion," I now regret not including you in that short list of dedications [in *Descent*]. There have been a good number of friends I might have included if I had taken more time and space with it. Anita Stelcel is not a "companion" in any true sense. She is, has been though briefly, a good friend with whom I have spent only a brief time last fall when she took me down to her cabin in Denali, and then the following day, on a great drive over the Denali Hwy to the McClaren [Maclaren] River, one of my favorite places in this part of Alaska, and where I had not been for several years. It was beautiful weather there in early September, and I remain grateful for Anita's making the time for it. She works a job at Prudhoe Bay, and has little time to spare for other things. I learned also that she has on a shelf at her home copies of all my books! I was rather amazed by that.

Anita's family comes from Estonia, but was raised in this country, in, I think, Chicago. But I am not familiar with all the details of her life, only what little she has told me. She was married, but is now divorced, has no children so far as I know. I have not seen her for some time now, but now and then I get an email from her at Prudhoe.

So, my dear Rachel, there you have it! As I said, there are other longtime friends I might have found some way to included in that brief dedication, but there is/was only a small amount of space I might have given to it. Again, I'm sorry I did not include you in another brief note. You merit it, one of the best friends I have found in this late time of life.

I did not mean to go on about this at such length, but I wanted answer your question and let you know that there is no one I value more as a friend at this late time of my life, than you, Lady Epstein. If I use the word "love" in writing to you, I mean it.

I want also to thank you once more for the gift of that hardcover edition of Rosa's writing on the Crisis in German Socialism, etc. Once more I am deeply impressed by her thought and writing. As I voiced it on my brief contribution to our meeting earlier this month, I want to say once more: "Rosa, come back ...!" We do indeed need her, or someone like her, at this time, or at any time in our increasingly corrupted political life.

So, Rachel, I hope I have answered your question, and added a deal more than you asked for!

Love,
John

Thank you for your good handwriting, by the way; I have no trouble in reading it.

As for the 9/11 letter, I understand your feeling about "innocence" and the other issues I raise and attempt to deal with. Incidentally, I sent a copy of the letter to the historian, Howard Zinn, who responded with enthusiastic support and agreement. I had not expected a response from him, and it was both a surprise and a gift to have that brief letter.

I am at this time of life alone most of the time, a fact I deal with and continue to function with, in my writing and everyday activity. Not easy at times, but given my years of age, not surprising or a calamity! This is one good and valid reason why the brief companionship of someone like Anita Stelcel can be as important as it is, or was. I have another old friend and former Montana student, Gretchen, who lives in Wasilla, teaches school in Palmer, and with whom I have spent time in recent years. Last fall her husband … was killed in a traffic accident in Anchorage, and that has been a terrible event for Gretchen. She has found comfort and relief in spending some time with me whenever there is a chance for it, and I also find some comfort in having her with me, if only briefly.

I hope this brief addition offers you a little understanding and consolation. Our lives are unpredictable, and a little love and companionship can at times be more than simply important.

---

2 April 10

Dear Rachel,

It has been hardly a week since I had your letter of March 24. I might have written back sooner, but I've been embedded with getting my tax figures together to give to my tax lady here, and I'm already late. But my troubled eyesight hasn't made any of this easier or better, and I guess that as a mentally crippled senior I can claim some extra time? I hope so.

I'm glad, of course, to know that you have <u>all</u> of my books, and they are safe from your cats. Tell me: do your cats read? If not, why would they bother with a book, except perhaps to have some paper to chew. Well, there are plenty of books these days that deserve a good chew, if nothing else. So, let the kitties have a go at it!

I believe I did see a review of the Hofstadter book you mentioned, but I have not read it. The British papers I subscribe to often have reviews of writers most of us here in the USA have never read or heard of...

My kidding aside, I want to thank you for your letter, your writing and your good words on my writing, and our friendship. Yes, it has been a rare and rewarding time for me, and it's good to know that my presence has been a similar thing for you. Not everyone, especially in academe, looks to John Haines for assurance and inspiration, etc. Some see me as a threat, an example of an independent spirit whose life and work might render their credentials as something of a classroom poster (or posture!). But I have nothing against an honest and informed teacher, and despite my years of being shunned by various English departments, I've survived and have done my work. Amen.

Now, as to your coming up here for a visit, that would be a treat for me. If you have no one up here you might stay with, you can stay with me if you don't mind sleeping on the couch! I have no spare bedroom, and the space is small, but you are welcome. Just, please, do not bring the cats! I have no place for them, no cellar hole or even an empty carton I might fill with dead leaves or old Xmas stuffing!

More seriously, I do think the 9/11 events remain volatile and potentially antagonistic, the major issues still unresolved to the extent that the event, the subject, as I described it in my brief piece, might be difficult to discuss in such a way that might clarify things like motives and a certain underlying justice in what happened. But perhaps one day it might be worth gathering at least a small group, professors, students, and citizens, for something like an open forum.

There are other possibilities, and I may mention one or two of them before I close off this letter. Without Rosa, we will be limited or handicapped no matter what we choose to discuss.

I have, incidentally, found a good piece of a plain white board on which I can mount one of the Rosa posters you sent me. I will have it here on my wall above my desk where I now sit and type. (My ribbon just wore out, and I had to replace it!)

Time is getting on, so I'll quit for the time being and finish this up in the morning. Good night, dear Racehl [sic]!

Later: In a new issue of the <u>Guardian</u> I found a brief article on what seems to be, in some places or schools, an attempt to get rid of laptops and their use in classrooms or elsewhere in schools. I will copy this and include it with my letter and card. Perhaps another subject to be discussed? (or disgusted!).

Another thought which I just recalled from a number of years ago:

"The teachers are everywhere.
What is wanted is a learner."

I found this [quote] in one of the writings of my old friend, Wendell Berry, and I discovered it when I was teaching at George Washington U. in Wash. DC. Well, I typed it up and posted it on my office door so that students and others might see it and read it. One of my English colleagues, Jody, saw it, and she printed it and posted it on doors and bulletin boards throughout the department! A nice surprise, though I can't affirm at this time if or not anyone, student or faculty, took it seriously enough to act on it. But keep it in mind, as I have.

Another subject or issue came to my attention on reading something in, or on a page of, the <u>NY Times</u> (I think). It was a critical piece on the lack of student's interest in history and the apparent lack of classes or courses that might correct this. Another subject worth some thought and discussion. I have noted myself a lack of any serious interest among students I have dealt with here, in politics and current state and national issues. I always bring this sort of thing to their attention and will ask them to resound to this or that subject or issue, current or past, or maybe future.

I type this sort of thing on cards and paper, in part because of my often failing handwriting. You write well by hand, ands I have no trouble in reading it. But it has become more and more difficult for me to simply write!

So, I will close this off and get it in the mail come Monday. Once more my eyesight is beginning to fail me, and I've said here about all I felt worth sending you for the time being. If I can think of additional subjects for a possible group discussion, I'll let you know of it in another letter.

It has been increasingly warm and clear here in the past week or more. The snow is melting, [there are] puddles and mud here and there, and maybe soon: Mosquitoes! Well, I hope not. There were few around here last summer.

Just let me know if you can make it up here for a visit. So far as I can see at this time, I will be here. I need to get back to the tax business, among other things.

Love to you and your cats. (Just don't let them read my books! Give them a page or two from the Bible, let them learn what it might be like to go to hell! Meow, Lord ...)

John

9 April 10

Dear Rachel,

In my last letter I mentioned this brief piece from <u>The Guardian</u>, and then I forgot to include a copy of it for your possible interest, as well as a few others down there at UAA. It's surprising to me that this happened at a school like GW, but it is also the more encouraging for that.

You are right, of course, that we need not feel obligated to respond to our letters, to and from, or only if we feel motivated by a particular subject or comment. I simply enjoy the exchange between us, and no one else writes as often as you do! So, write when you wish to, and I will do the same. I assume that neither Brian or your cats are jealous of our familiarity as expressed in a letter, and in your case, hand-written!

Anyway, I very much appreciated the card that you sent with the copy of "Parabola," a publication I had not seen before that I can recall. Thanks for sending it, a very impressive magazine (if that is the right word for it). I especially liked reading the piece by Helen Keller, something I had not seen before, though I know her name and now something of her writing. I also liked the story by Oscar Wilde, another piece I had not seen or heard of, though I've read some of his work. And, the excerpt from Joyce's "The Dead," a story I know, have read, and have seen also the film based on it.

And thanks also for your thought, or concern about my financial situation, whether pending or actual. I did not expect Kathy to do anything about this personally, but thought she might at least keep it in mind if some possibility of assistance appeared among the circuits.

I finally handed in my tax forms yesterday, and will await comment from the agent I have depended on since the early 1980s. She knows my situation, and I can depend on her concern for my best options, etc. I'm lucky, as I well know, and I do my best to refrain from complaints!

So, I'll get this in the mail tomorrow, and you can reply if and when you feel like it!

Love,
John

PS: Just as I was about to leave UAA and the bookstore last month, you showed me a copy of the video on Rosa, the film we have talked about.

Was it yours, or from the UA library? I still hope to see it once more, and to get it in the DVD!

<u>Guardian Weekly</u>,
2-9 April 2010
"Laptops no longer welcome"

> ......Professors have banned laptops from their classroom at George Washington University, American University, and the University of Virginia, among many others. Last month, a physics professor at the University of Oklahoma poured liquid nitrogen on to a laptop and then shattered it on the floor, a warning to the digitally distracted...

—Daniel de Vise, *Washington Post*

18 April 10

Dear Rachel,

Just a note to let you know that I have posted <u>Rosa</u> above my desk, and I turn to the left, there she is, looking right down on me! I finally got it taped and pinned together, and though less than perfect, I'm glad to have it there. Thank you for sending me those lovely, striking posters. I will try to get one framed and mounted in a better way.

No need to respond to this, though you know I always love getting something from you. I will have more news later (he said), but for the moment my thanks as always.

  Love,
  John

28 April 10

Dear Rachel,

Thank you for the latest card and note, which I have misplaced somewhere and have not so far found! But it is always good to have something from you. I did have a letter from Tom, [Tom Sexton established the UAA English Department in 1970, was Alaska Writer Laureate from 1995-2000] telling me he had met with you for coffee, and very much enjoyed talking to you; that you are a very intelligent person and a good talker! (As if I did not know that!)

I am writing in concern as to a couple of projects that lie in waiting for me. I still plan to come down to Anchorage and retrieve that storage stuff I've mentioned more than once. Now that the winter is gone, the snow and cold, it is time I did it, got it over with. I'll need help, for sure, and if you are available that would make things even better and easier for me. But I'll need to find someone, and if you are for some reason not able to be on hand, I'll have to look elsewhere. But there is time, and perhaps next month, or in June? Time enough to make plans for it.

The other subject is something quite a surprise. A friend of mine, a reader of my work, who lives in Illinois, retired from teaching, has put together something he has called: "A Tribute to John Haines" for an AWP meeting in Washington next February. I have no details as yet, but he has been able to gather a small group of old friends and fellow poets who will speak for me and my years of writing; and time will be allowed for me to read a few poems, a piece of prose, etc. My friend, Bruce Guernsey, has told me he will be able to have my expenses paid, and I'm glad for that; otherwise, it's not likely I would be able to be there. This has been quite a surprise, something I would never have expected. I am not a fan of the AWP (Association of Writers & Writing Programs), and I am not very popular among the tenured crew that more or less dominate these things. But Bruce is a good man, and I'm sure things will work out well with his command of it.

I would not expect you, or Kathy, or Sexton, etc., to be there, but I wanted to tell you of it in case there are some folks there, or here, who might make plans to come East for a day or two, and to honor the old, Elder Alaska poet! So, we'll see how it goes, and if or not I am still here (in the true sense) and able to take part in it.

So, another piece of news from the Frontier (or Back-tier)! I'm still working some things out here and waiting for the tax news, etc.

I look forward to seeing you again.

Love,
John

---

6 May 10

Dear Rachel,

Here is a copy of the email I had last week from my friend, Bruce Guernsey, who has proposed and prepared the AWP event in Washington next year. You'll see a list of the people who will be part of it, all friends of mine except for Sheryl St. Germain, whose name I recognize but cannot recall having met her.

Of course, as Bruce says, it still has to be approved by the AWP folks, etc., but not likely they will turn it down. Not something I might have expected, and I'm not a fan of the writing programs that have more or less conquered the art, but if things work out, I look forward to being there, and it will be good also to see Kathy if she comes to it, as you say she does.

Thanks for the card, and I'm glad to meet another House Mouse! Well, I can imagine it as pretty risky with your cats prowling the rooms, on watch for a mouse to bite! But I'm a damned big Mouse, and I don't take no shit from cats!

I like the idea of the bookstore history meetings, if it works out. Please keep me posted on this, and if I could make it, I'd like to sit in on one of the meetings. Of course, I will bring Rosa with me! I've read a lot of history in these past decades, and I can mention the Swiss writer and thinker, Jacob Burckhardt, whose books I kept with me while still at the homestead. [Swiss historian Jacob Burckhardt (1818-1897), author of *The Civilization of the Renaissance in Italy* and *Force and Freedom: Reflections on History.* He originated and professed the study of cultural history within art history.]

Thank you for staying in touch, Rachel. I'll let you know when and if I can make it down there, with some place to stay and some good help. I may mention this to Tom Sexton also, since he has a house down there and most likely be there and on hand if I need his help.

Well, after some very nice warm days during the past weeks, yesterday came a cold snowfall, wet and nasty. Hard to believe, with snow still sticking on the tree limbs here and the porch floor like a slick skating rink...

    Love,
    John

[Enclosed Bruce Guernsey email]

2010-04-29 Haines-mail

From: bruce guernsey [...]
Date: Sun, Apr 25, 2010 at 2:26 PM
Subject: Re: Phone number
To: John Haines jmhaines@alaska.edu

Dear John,

We are all set up now for the tribute next February. However, this is not the Library of Congress but the Associated Writers' Program (AWP) conference scheduled for next February 2-5 in D.C.

The conference is a big deal and there will be lots of writers there from all over the country, and you and the panel should have a very big audience.

Here are the participants (they allow six in all): you, me (as organizer and moderator), Steve Rogers, Baron Wormser, Dana Gioia, and Sheryl St. Germain. Sheryl's name might surprise you some, but she is a huge fan of your work and is using your essay "Snow" in her anthology. She also runs an MFA program that is based on writing about nature and the wilderness.

The application must still be approved by AWP, but I can't imagine they will turn us down. My next chore will be to raise some money for expenses—for your flight and hotel, primarily.

Thanks for the phone number. I'll have this all submitted by tomorrow PM. We leave for Maine on May 4, and I have to get busy packing.

Best, as ever—Bruce

Dr. Bruce Guernsey
Distinguished Professor Emeritus
Eastern Illinois University
and Editor, "The Spoon River Poetry Review"
www.bruceguernsey.com

17 May 10

Dear Rachel,

I still hope you can make it up here for a visit, but I understand that might not be possible for you. As for my coming down there for the storage stuff, I hope to be more specific about next month.

I am, have been for the past some days, in a very bad situation, unable to drive my car, dependent on friends to come and take me where I need to go for one reason or another. A complicated story, but my driving license is expired and I may find myself under arrest or in jail if I take the chance and go out in the car. But I can tell you more later. It has left me depressed and frustrated, unable to post the mail I need to send. I had hoped that with age on me I might find some basic things easier to take care, deal with, etc., but that ain't the way it is.

Anyway, a really nice day up here, soon to be in the 70s, or so they say. We need some rain, or there may be a bad fire season ahead.

I sent Kathy a letter in answer to hers not long ago. And I continue to think of that "History" meeting you have promoted. I may not be able to be there, but good luck with it. As you see in the face of this card, I still write!

Love,
John

24 May 10

Dear Rachel,

Thanks for your note and the ADN [*Anchorage Daily News*] article which I have not read well so far, just skimmed through. But I wanted to respond to your question re my driving license. It's a longtime problem, dating back to my time living in Montana in the late '90s. I made a serious mistake in trading my Alaska license for a Montana license. Then came later a major event with a partially blocked artery that struck me with acute pain and sent me to the hospital in Missoula. It wasn't a heart attack, but it might have resulted in one eventually. I had the good fortune of a cardiologist who performed a stent procedure to relieve the artery blockage. It worked very well, and I've had no real pain since.

Well, it happened that a young intern MD there learned of my event, and called the State DMV and, however he did it, he asked them to cancel my driver's license, a major surprise for me, or a shock. Meanwhile the doctor who performed my stent procedure, affirmed that I was safe to drive, but for some weird reason the DMV office refused his written testimony. So, since then I have driven without a valid license, rented a car when I was back east for several months in 2006-7, and drove without mishap or apparent violation...very careful, of course. When I came back to Fairbanks in 2007, I decided to try and renew my Alaska license. I went with a friend to the local Vehicle office and applied. I passed the test, the paper work, without any trouble. Then the gal behind the desk, searching the internet, discovered the Montana incident, and I learned that my Alaska license would be refused. And that's how it's been until just recently.

And then, another weird experience. I went up to the UA Honors House one day, to check on mail and email, and parked outside as usual, but too close to the car belonging to the office staff. I came back out, intending to move out and get myself back to the house here. Well, she came out also, and I was too close to allow her access to her driver's side of her car. In backing out to give her room, my side mirror slightly scraped the door of her car, but leaving no scratch or any sign of damage. But she ... flew into a rage, yelling at me, and then with her cell phone called a campus police officer. He came, and one thing led to another, with me being treated like a convicted criminal. He spoke of putting me under arrest, or in jail, but that didn't happen. I was, however, given a citation, and told that I must appear in court this coming Friday.

So, that's pretty much the story. I blame myself, but the incident was not a major one, and it would not have come to anything serious had it not been revealed that I had been driving with an expired license.

What may come of this, I don't know, but I hope to have it resolved without a jail sentence, and perhaps as a result of all this regain my Alaska license! Or so I hope. I can of course, continue to drive, being careful to avoid any police cars, etc.! But it's a difficult problem, and I am very much in need of my car. I am now dependent on friends taking me where I need to go, or as today, calling a cab and paying for that.

So, now you have it. I'm sorry to have taken up so much space on this paper, but hope you understand the situation. If you think of any means of help for me, let me know. I am not happy about the court appearance, but I dare not avoid it! There should be some way to resolve all of this, and not leave me a criminal. But I'll let you know the outcome, or maybe it will show up in the newspaper!

Love,
John

(I have an attorney down there in Anchorage: Peter Grinder. He might be of some help in this trouble I face.)

[Enclosed typed index card]

Rachel: Something else I forgot to
mention: There was an article/review of
a book in the local Sunday Paper, written
by a friend, Mike Dunham, who has worked
for the Anchorage paper for many years.
I would like to contact him, but do not

have an address. If you can find it in
the city phone book, please send it on to
me. I would like for him to review this
new book, and I think he might do it.

John

[Enclosed, picture of a cat painting:
a mural of cat-angels with trumpet
and harp by cartoonist B. Kliban.]

1 Jun 10

Dear Rachel,

    Here is the item I spoke of not long ago when you called, and I had intended to simply hand it on to you when you stopped by for a visit. But since you have postponed that, I am sending it on by mail. I found it amusing, and thought you would also. Perhaps one of your cats will get a laugh from it!

    Anyway, I look forward to seeing you here, if only briefly, and to meeting Brian also. I hope to be here, not in jail nor in some more complicated situation and with no solution in sight. It is more than simply irritating, and I have myself to blame for it, in great part due to my move to Montana some years ago, and then my mistaken decision to discard my Alaska driver's license for a new Montana license. A complicated story, and I will not attempt a detailed account of it here. Enjoy the cat artist's brush work! Could be a masterpiece, with GW Bush among the faces!

    Love,
    John

6 June 10

Dear Rachel,

Thanks for the Cat-card, which I recall seeing on a rack more than once. I'm sorry I haven't one at hand ...

I wish you were to be up here for a visit this weekend; I need the company, and no one has returned a call today. But I had a good day yesterday, some shopping with an old friend. It's just damned lonely for me here at this time, and with no way yet to resolve the predicament I find myself in. I do take a chance and drive down to Campus Corner now and then, as I did today, to pick up a copy of the <u>Sunday-Times</u> and maybe another item or two.

Well, I did have a call from a former student, and he came over to take me down to the campus and to my old office, a nice surprise, and I feel the better for it. So, now, back to this card and letter.

I have in fact an application to what is called <u>Van Tran</u>, a public means of transport for seniors and handicapped. I ain't a cripple yet, and I still prefer to drive my car; but under the circumstances it will be best to have an alternative. Not easy to get used to being an elder needing help!

I read a review of <u>Legends of a Suicide</u> in the local Sunday paper not long ago, and it sounded to me worth reading, though I haven't a copy of it and no plans to buy one yet. I have all too much to read as it is, and my eyesight makes it all increasingly difficult. But thanks for mentioning it, and I may look for it in the local bookstore one day soon. My father suffered a good deal in his age, with Alzheimer's and a blood problem that finally put him down, to be laid to rest in Arlington Cemetery. When I last saw him before he died, he did not know who I was and had nothing to say to me. And then, after having spent a night at his place in DC, with his wife, Mabel, a public nurse, he suddenly woke up and spoke my name: "Jack, Jack..." as I was called when I was a kid. A moving occasion, for both of us.

Yes, Kooistra and I have been friends for many years, having met at one time or another, in one place or another. He first stopped at the homestead in 1966, still a student at a university back east. He had found a copy of my <u>Winter News,</u> and wanted to see the place itself, meet the author.

Well, I have been able to do a couple of things this day, Sunday, and am feeling ready to go back to bed. It is always good to have a card or letter from you, so don't quit on it! Bring your cats, and we'll find a squirrel or a mouse for them to play with!

Love,
John

ಹ

6/13/10

Dear Rachel,

I got your recent card and as always enjoyed reading it, thinking of answers to your questions. The book I have of Burckhardt's, <u>Reflections on History</u>, was originally titled <u>Force and Freedom</u>, the same that you have mentioned. I found it in a library, but when I looked to buy a copy I learned of the title change. But it is the same book, and I'm glad you are reading it. On looking into my copy, I find so many passages that I marked from page to page, to return to or copy for some class I might teach.

I know nothing of Raymond Williams [Welsh writer and intellectual, 1921-1988, author of *Culture and Society]* or Perry Anderson [British historian, born 1938, author of *Considerations on Western Marxism*], but I will make note of their names and perhaps look them up on some library shelf—that is, if I can still read! My eyes are more and more troubled, and I don't know what the trouble is, except for age.

I called Mike Dunham after getting your card, left a message and last night he called back. It was good to hear him after a pretty long time, and he told me that he did have the copy of my book [*Descent*], was reading it, and might write a review of it. [In John's handwriting:] *If you could get a mail address for Mike Dunham, I would appreciate it.* So, that is good news, and I'll hope that he does write at least some brief notice on it.

As for your question re e-books, I am not at all in favor of this, and I do not want my books made into some Google fashion objects. If this might encourage readers to buy copies of the real book, that might make it worthwhile. But when I stop off as I did this morning at the College Coffee House to get a copy of the <u>NY Times</u>, and I see so many people there reading their laptops, I am not at all cheered by the thought of "readers" etc. Not often do I see a student on campus with a <u>book</u>!

Well, I am otherwise feeling a bit better about my driving problem and forthcoming appearance in court. I just had a letter from an appointed Public Defender, and I will give him, or her, the story as I know it. I no longer feel under threat of being jailed, but I do want my driving rights restored as soon as they can be. I have applied for some public transit for elders and handicapped people, but I prefer to drive myself when I want to and wherever I need to go. I have good friends here, former students, who have been very kind in stopping by to take me where I need to go, for shopping, postal needs, and so forth. But again, I want the use of my car! Dammit!

And there remains the need to take care of somethings down there in Anchorage or area, and I'll be waiting to deal with that.

So, that's about it for this Sunday mid-day. Thanks again for writing, and I'll be in touch if anything turns up (or down!).

Love,
John

<u>PS</u>: I wish you were closer, so we could talk about things like Jacob B. his life and his work, and related things.

I want to ask you to check on a possible Hemlock Society there in Anchorage. I want to contact them, if possible, ask for some information, details, etc. If you find a phone number for this, please send it on to me, and do not be alarmed by my request!

When I was last down in Anchorage, for the Rosa event, you showed me a copy of the film on her life and work. Was that your copy, or the library's? I still want to encourage someone to get a DVD edition of it made, and I'm sure it can be done—it IS done with many other films from the 1930s, '40s,'50s, etc. Just a matter of promoting it to the right person in the right place.

24 June 10

Dear Rachel,

Thank you so much for the card and all that you had to say—but then, in another packet, the Rosa film! I was most moved to open it up and see that face and the title, and to read all the rest on the film packet. Dear God, I so want to see that film again, but here I am and without the means for it at hand. But I am going to show this to someone at Blockbuster and urge them to try and get it into a DVD form; I know it can be done and should be done. I will also take the movie to the UAF library and make a similar proposal (or demand!). I think we'll get it, and it may take some time.

Is the film yours? Do you want it returned? Just let me know.

Your mention of "great books" is not elitist, not at all. It is something I have been witness to in many classes in recent years: the readers, young and old, simply do not read the great works, or not often, faced into the typical mediocre page so common now. I always introduce to students parts of writing I know is what they need to read, whether verse, essay, or fiction; not many, however, follow up on it. But I will not cease to point the way, whether in English, German, Spanish, Russian, whatever I can cite, quote from, etc.

Thank you also for Mike Dunham's address; I will write to him and maybe prompt him to write a decent review of DESCENT; it surely deserves something in one of our local papers.

I ain't got no cat poems handy, but I'm sure there are a few out there, and not all for kids, either. I know I have read one or two in the past some months, a year or so, but I can't quote from it at this time.

Yes, my B-day is due next week, but I'm not looking forward to it; the years are increasingly a pain, and I'd just as soon turn back the clock and celebrate my 65th! Things here remain difficult re the driver license problem, and I will have to talk with my Public Defender woman again and soon. Too complicated a matter to deal with here. Thank you once more for writing, and sending...

    Love,
    John

[ENCLOSED NOTECARD]

Madison Park Greetings

"A REAL FRIEND IS ONE WHO WALKS IN
WHEN THE REST OF THE WORLD WALKS OUT."
    Walter Winchell

[In John's handwriting:]
AND THAT'S YOU, DEAR RACHEL,
    FOR SURE!

9 July 10

Dear Rachel,

Thank you once more for the card and letter. I look for these from you, and behold: it appears in the box!

My birthday was mostly a day of moaning. I had contracted some weird illness that seems to be going around: coughing, sinus congestion, eye-watering, sneezing, etc. It is still with me, but not as bad as it was. Just what it is, no one seems to know, but it has been exhausting for me, and I know it has for others, including my next-door landlord. So, the b-day went by, though I was taken to an early evening gathering of local people on Sunday, and that was nice, though I tired quite early and was taken home.

I've not been able to do anything with the Rosa film yet, but I intend to visit with the UA librarian and see what might be possible. I did take it to a local Blockbuster I go to for a movie once a week, but whether anything may come of that I can't say. But again, I will not give up on it. Thanks for making it a gift and not just a loan. I will keep it with care, and find an occasion to watch it once more.

My trial, as you call it, is due on July 19, but I will not be required to be there. My Public Defender will be there on my behalf and with my signed agreement. I'm glad she suggested we do it this way and save me more courthouse trouble—my hearing defect, for one thing!

I have read reviews of Stieg Larsson's work, but I've read none of his books so far. I may seek one out for a look. I am at this time reading a collection of stories by Irene Nemirovsky, just recently published by Vintage Press: DIMANCHE, translated from the French. I have very much enjoyed the stories, and glad I found a copy of it just incidentally at the local bookstore. I had not seen a review of it.

I'm making best use of the time I have and while it is summer. I still hope to come down there for a visit, and since you apparently do not plan to come up here. I have to make some plans for the coming fall and winter, and will let you know more when I do! Do stay in touch; your cards mean a lot.

 Love,
 John

                 21 July 10

Dear Rachel,

 Thanks as always, for your cattie card and letter! Them fancy, smug kitties, so proud of themselves and for no good reason! Just good old American urban egos, etc.

 But I agree with your impression of these stage performers and their sneaky pride in reading from their work and not quitting when the assigned time is up. I saw, heard, a sample of this at the Library of Congress a few years ago: the poet dressed nicely, like a local business executive, with numerous curtsies to the audience and a smug smile, and so forth. Well, I ain't like that, though I also read at the Library a few years ago, on the platform for at least an hour, and when I was done, I could hardly move! My feets felt nailed to the stage. But it was apparently a successful event, and the director of the reading series told me that it was the best read she had heard in her time at the LOC! A nice bit of news, and I'm sure she meant it, not just a bit of formal praise. Ah well, the politics of performer art, and there seems no end to it. Thanks for the reminder, and I know that not all of my contemporaries are among the self-appointed, etc.

 You will probably not get this card until you return from Californicator. I hope you have a good time of it down there, with family, etc.

As for my reading of Irene Nemirovsky, the impression I had from the stories in <u>Dimanche</u> sent me back to the other collections of her writing, and I've been very impressed by it all. I have not gone back to <u>Suite Francaise</u> yet, but I may begin on that one once more when I have finished reading the rest of the work I have with me here. That work is a much longer story (unfinished, as you know) than the collected stories I've been reading. I have since considered turning to a writing of short fiction, something I have not yet attempted, though I love to tell stories, have done so in my many memoirs of the homestead years and other times in my life. Maybe not, but I'll wait to see, and if I can continue to write! Well, I do write letters, as you know all too well, you and many others among my friends.

As for my possible move from here to Southcentral, to Wasilla, I await word from my old friend down there, who has been on a major European trip with her son during the past month, and will soon be home. She will need to prepare for her teaching at a school in Palmer. So we'll see how it goes, and if or not I can manage a visit down there to check things out. I'll let you and others know...Not an easy decision, but maybe the right one ...

Have a good visit down there.

 Love,
 John

ཨ⁓

14 Aug 2010

Dear Rachel,

As always, your cards, notes, letters, are a boost to my sometimes lagging spirits...So, once more, my thanks.

I have a request: if you still have, or can find, the Mike Dunham comment, or quote, on my DESCENT, I would like to see it, if you can send it on to me. I don't often look into the "Big City" paper, but I know that sometimes there are items worth reading. I'm glad to know that Mike at least made some mention of the book for a few readers down there.

I am very glad to have your quote from "Shadows," ["Shadows II"], one of the most cherished essays. The passage you quote, incidentally, is from section III of the essay, not II. [The essay published in *We Make A Fire*, Orca Press 1982, edited by Cheryl Morse, is "Shadows II".] There is a lot of thought and memory in those pages, nourished by my reading at the time. I worked on it for a long time, but the writing and rewriting was worth it. Thanks for quoting from it and for reading it. I have not seen a bat for a long time, and none here so far.

Thanks, by the way, for your thoughts on the possibility of me writing some fiction. Maybe, but the time is getting short for me, and I am dealing with increasing limits.

One thing I have done lately is to have made a small collection of photos from my early days here, 1947-48, and my building of the first homestead cabin with the help of a few older carpenter friends. I had forgotten I had kept this ancient photo album for so many years, and then recently I found it in one of the boxes I kept in my Honors office at UAF. It was quite a discovery, and one or two friends to whom I showed the collection have been quite taken by it. So, I decided to have some decent copies made of the best of them, and I plan to mail a couple of the copied pages to a former student friend here, and to my literary trustee, Steve Rogers, back east. I know he'll treasure it and make some worthwhile use of it when I am gone and the story needs to be told, in full!

I went for my Saturday lap swim, which is always a good thing; but my eyes are fading as I type this letter, and I'll have to quit and get to bed soon. Thank you again for writing and staying in touch; it means a lot to this elder gent. I'll let you know when or if I decide to come to Anchorage, or somewhere in the area.

 Love,
 John

(I may be going "batty")

                 27 Aug 10

Dear Madam Blackfoot:

 I got your white-printed card not long and ago, and as always am glad to hear from you. I had no trouble reading your nicely printed white toe-tracks, but as you suggest, I await something on Whiteman paper!

 Well, I am not familiar with Gond art, though I think I have seen that word before. When I first read your letter, I wasn't sure what you were talking about, or if there was simply a misprint on your part. But if you can send me a copy or two of something in this art, I would like to see it. As you must know, I am a serious former artist, someone who finally chose the art of poetry to devote his life to, but the visual imagery of this life and art remains for me a serious matter, and at times a source of poetry.

 Yes, I do still plan to come down to Anchor-wage, but have no date for it yet. A matter of getting there and paying for it. I can't drive the distance anymore…So, I'll let you know, if and when.

 I have no trouble with anthologies, depending on the contents, and the same is true of journals, reviews, etc. I do recall the <u>Orca</u> issue you mention, ["Shadows II"] but I haven't seen a copy of it for some time. I remember the folks who started that journal and did well. The card you wrote on and sent me is quite a thing to look at, and the tree on the cover image is quite a thing to look at. I will keep the card, and if you have access to any others I'd like to see one.

I assume you will remain with the bookstore, not teaching a class? I will miss spending time with my students this fall, but I have too much to do, and the time is getting on. I simply want to go to sleep and let the world and its men and monkeys get on with their silly chatter, but leave me alone!

I have been rereading the work of Irene Nemirovsky lately, all of her books which I have, and am presently deep into the major work, Suite Francaise. I had forgotten parts of the story, but it is coming back to me, and I remain very much in admiration of the woman, her life and her work.

So, that's about it for the moment. My eyesight is giving me trouble once more, and it is getting late in the evening. I'll be in touch, and will look for another card from you.

Love,
John

PS: You mentioned reading journals, anthologies, etc. Just yesterday I found a copy of the Spring 2004 issue of The Hudson Review, which I have read and subscribed to for many years, and which has published a lot of my work over the years. I found in it at least two reviews I had somehow missed reading before: one on Yeats [the great Irish poet William Butler Yeats (1865-1939)], the other on the Greek writer, George Seferis [(1900-1971)]. I began reading the piece on Yeats this morning, and will take up the other review tomorrow. So, the lesson here is that you can never be certain you have read everything in any given issue, whether paper, magazine, or journal. It is always worth going back for a look ...

Love,
John

LIMERICK

One Sunday, feeling unfed,
I took a fat Turkey to bed.
In our love-making state
She's been losing some weight,
And the Turkey and I are now wed!

—John Haines, 2009

17 Sept 2010

Dear Rachel,

I wrote the above verse some time ago and had forgotten it. And then today, while looking through some pages of a listing of things, I discovered the verse, and it gave me a good laugh and some cheer as of this morning. What prompted it, I don't know, but I am always alert to occasions to write something "light," to amuse myself and maybe a friend or two, though in some cases I think the verse worth getting printed. Well, we [we'll] see...maybe.

But I want to thank you for the recent packet of things you sent me with your nice letter. I did like the Gond cards, and I will send them off to a friend or two with a greeting in "White" ink! Seriously, it is something very new for me. I very much liked the colored pages of the various art work, and if you have still some of the cards, there is one or two I would like to see, to have, such as the DB Khirsali white (or black). I refer to the cards, of course, not the artwork. Anyway, quite a collection of images and of which I knew little or nothing before. You folks there in the UAA bookstore are lucky to meet up with this sort of thing.

Words, Writings, and Letters

I wanted to get this brief note in the mail before you left for DC. [I attended the Library of Congress National Book Festival representing Alaska for Alaska Center for the Book.] There is nothing I can think of that you might get for me back there, except maybe a decent replacement for Lady Lisa [Senator Lisa Murkowski]. I doubt Joe Miller [Libertarian candidate for Senate] will be much better; as I read of his designs for this or that, I think that things can only get worse ...

I have no plans to write anything about the "Suite" story. I finished reading it, as well as all the other books by Nemirovsky I have here. There is one, referred to in a review I read last year: <u>The Dogs and the Wolves</u>, and which I've been unable to find in this country. Maybe it will show, be available, eventually.

The Wasilla venture remains uncertain at this time. I've had no word from my friend Gretchen, and I will need a lot of help in getting things packed up for the move. I hope to confirm it one way or another, soon.

I had a letter from Charlotte Fox at the State Arts Council, letting me know that they were preparing to pay my way east in February for the AWP event. That was good news, as I could not afford the trip otherwise. Too bad your DC visit won't happen at that time; we could spend a bit of time there in the city; I could show you a few things and places you might not see otherwise.

Anyway, I'll let you know how things go, and if I also go! The time and the age does get on, and I live more and more within the limits.

So, enjoy Chicago, [I planned to visit my brother on the way back from DC] say hello to Carl Sandburg if or when you see him! Don't hang out in that damned O-Hare airport...You'll die of something there, for sure.

Love,
John

[ENCLOSED NOTECARD]

Anne Tainof
(A woman, dressed as a housewife from the '50s, holding a tabby cat, with the words: *it was the best rebound relationship ever!*)

6 Oct 2010

Dear Rachel,

Your card arrived here on Monday (not from Washington, mind you), and it was nice once more to hear from you. You did not mention the card/letter I sent you last month, with the limerick typed at the head of the page. Perhaps you didn't get it? Let me know, and I'll send on a copy of it.

There is nothing you can send me that I can think of, except a retirement fund, a cozy nest to live in, and a nice young house-maid for company! How does that sound?

Well, to speak more seriously, things here are about the same. I am unemployed, without retirement, but still able to drive (avoid long-distance), and I go shopping once or twice a week. I continue to read (not easy), and respond to the letters I receive from friends like you. A couple of times a week I watch a decent film, mainly foreign, and give my eyes a rest from reading. I recently had a brief visit with an old friend from DC, a former student who now lives a part of the year at her home place in West Virginia, but works in Washington also. Her husband is French, and she spends a holiday over there with him and his family. She was here on a visit with another local friend whom she knows, having met him through me a good many years ago.

I can't say I'm excited about the event in DC, though I very much appreciate my friend, Bruce [Guernsey], working to make it possible. I do look forward to seeing a bit of Washington once more, and my old school neighborhood near Dupont Circle. But there won't be a lot of time to roam around the city, visit museums, etc. And I will have to be careful and not overdue things, run up bills, expenses, etc. I rather wish it were taking place at a warmer time of the year here. I may get my flight here in Fairbanks with the temps maybe 40 below zero!

All I know of Chicago is what I have seen while waiting a flight change. I may have spent a bit more time there years ago when the family was changing trains on the way West, or East. But I am not a skyscraper fan, and I can't say I missed the Trade Towers after the event of 9/11. I prefer a church, or one of the old London parliament bldgs.

But I'm glad you are back, and I hope to see you once more when I do get down to Anchorage or Wasilla/Palmer, etc. I thought of you and your cats when I saw this card, and the enclosed cartoon copy gave me a laugh. Meow!...

Love,
John

23 Oct 2010

Dear Rachel,

Well, another Cat-card! I keep looking for them to send to you, since you seem so catty. But thanks for the two good letter-cards I had from you not long ago. Time goes by sooner than I can keep track of, it seems, and I often find myself farther behind in responding than I had expected.

I can't respond to all that you asked about, not without some further thought and a break from the excess I find myself taken up with. I would like to have been there for the two readings you mentioned. [Poet Anne Coray author of *Violet Transparent*, 2010; *Bone Strings*, 2005; and Steve Kahn author of *The Hard Way Home: Alaska Stories of Adventure, Friendship, and the Hunt, 2010*] Was this a bookstore?... it would have been a nice break from things here (silence and isolation). Last week Nancy Lord was here to give a talk, and I forgot to make time for it. I had sent her a copy of my DESCENT, and look forward to hearing from her when she's had time to read some of it. She's a fine writer, and I very much like her personally. She's a bit shy of me, I think, due to my senior status as writer, etc. She's not alone in that, I think.

To answer one question: I have more than once been involved in a romance with someone younger than me, whether a former student or a new friend, and for one reason or another have been left behind, traded for someone younger or more financially or circumstantially stable. If you've read some of my memoir stories you will have met with some of what I refer to. I was indeed a romantic when I was younger, steeped in the poetry of certain periods, and simply in search of the right person or woman, younger or not. There are poems from my younger years, in my collection, <u>At the End of This Summer, Poems 1948-1954</u>, which tell the story as I was able to tell it at that time. I guess something of that time and mood still lingers in this elder I've become ... To have some decent company, a friendship in which affection has its place, is a welcome for me, always.

I can tell you that my first wife, Peggy Davis, remains a close friend. We met as art students in New York in 1950, were married a year later, and moved out to California in 1952, a long story, but I will not tell it all here. In 1954 I packed things up, and drove us up to Alaska, to my homestead here, and which I knew I needed to reclaim and begin a new life. Well, Alaska was not for Peg. She wanted New York, and after two years with me at the homestead she returned to Manhattan. That's where she's been, still is. I understood, and felt no anger over it, but it was lonely there, at Mile 68, me and the three or four dogs I then had. There is more to the story, but I won't tell it all here. If I am ever in New York I make time to see Peg, spend a little time together, sometimes a night in her fancy apartment overlooking the East River. She inherited money from her father's estate when he died, and it has allowed her to live as she has wished. Now and then she sends me a check, and I am always grateful for that.

So, there you have a part of the story, but it ain't all of it and won't be. I hope you at least now have a better picture of things as this life has been for me.

My eyes are getting tired, so I'd best sign off on this for the time being. At some point (with a little kitty in my lap) I'll tell more of the story. I liked the two cards you sent, and I hope this one I'm sending at least amuses you. You can give your Brian my regards. It seems to me that the two of you are lucky being together, but that doesn't stop me from sending...

Love, as always...

John

PS: No one writes to me as well and as often as you, Rachel. It is always a deep pleasure to find another card & letter in the box from you. No one else, with advent and convenience of e-mail, does this. So, please don't quit on it, but also don't take it as an obligation. I'm an elder writer at this point in time, perhaps nearing the end of an unusual career or, better, a vocation, a lifetime commitment to the art of Letters.

Once more, thank you for this long lasting friendship...

John

[ENCLOSED NOTECARD]

AVANTI PRESS, INC.
Photo: Allen Wallace
Photo of a cat sitting at a bar, licking its paw, with salt, a lime wedge, half a shot of milk, and a milk bottle with milk on the bar.
Another year...shot!

[John typed:]
HMMM ...Well, maybe a little sip of Vodka? I can imagine Russian cats taking a snort, so why not me!

[No date on card, envelope stamped Nov 8, 2010]

[In John's handwriting:] *Dear Rachel,*

Well, another Cat-card for you. I do enjoy looking through the shop files, and maybe finding something that will give you a chuckle. And truth is, I need a little humor at this time. Last week I paid a visit with my physician, very much in need of help ... a bad aching system over all, and no remedy in sight. Things are a bit better as I write this. At this age one never knows what might show up next.

But, yes, I would like to see the piece you mentioned, on Sarah Palin [Governor of Alaska 2006-2009, 2010 Republican Vice-President candidate]. And what think you of the election outcomes? I voted, as always, but not for Joe or Lisa ... No thanks!

I don't want to overload you, Rachel, with my cards and letters, but it means a great deal to me at this time to have something from you, always so well written and also often humorous. So please do not give up on it, or me.

I am still in conflict with myself as to a move south, whether to Wasilla/Palmer, or maybe Juneau. My good friend, Cindy Smith, who lives down there, has worked for the state and has been a good friend to me, has recently written me on various Pioneer Homes, and I am still thinking about that option, providing of course, there might be room for me in one of the places. It's just not easy for me to make the decision and resign myself to the move.

I met with a young student from Israel today on a brief visit to the Honors House and a look into my former office space, which I miss. A nice young fellow, and we had a brief conversation on one thing or another…

I've another Cat-card on hand, but will save it for a later time. Meanwhile, I'll look to hear from you once more when you feel like writing.

Love, and my best,
John

ଏ୬

22 Nov 2010

Dear Rachel,

Another card, but no more Cats for a week or two. I pick these various cards from the local bookstore, and find many of them pretty rare in their quoting from intelligent folks.

I did get the card with the poem and the article on homelessness. I will read the piece once more when I get a break from other readings, etc. I know what homelessness is or can be, and have written on it, as I think you know: "On the Street."

I wish I could attend some of your bookstore events; it doesn't happen here, not at UAF that I know of, or seldom. Plenty of work for folks like you, I'm sure, but worth the time, effort? I hope so.

What I might say to anyone with a dull life and little talent: Read! Check out the library shelves if you don't want to buy a book: classics, Greek and Roman, English Lit, modern or earlier. Learn to read another language: Spanish, German, etc. Read aloud to yourself, listen to the words there on the page and in your ear. Memorize lines and passages from poems; and read slowly, not to skim a page or paragraph and move on to another dull "bestseller."

Well, as you say, not every story needs to be written, but that choice is up to the potential writer—if there is one!

This past Sunday <u>Times Magazine</u> has a lengthy piece on Sarah Palin, her life and political activities. I did not read it, have little serious interest in the woman and her obvious ambitions. Had she stayed with the governor's job, did the needed work, put her ambitions aside for at least the time being, I might vote for her in a future election. She ain't dumb, just a self-acclaimed star. So, what think you of her and her activities? She might, just might, end up in a presidential race. Well, excuse me, Sarah, I must leave the country!

Well, I've plenty to do, and at times my energies simply are not up to it. But so far at least I remain active in one thing or another, and with plenty still to do, though another book seems unlikely.

I had a nice surprise in the mail last week. The editor of the <u>Hampden-Sydney Poetry Review</u> (in Virginia) sent me a short letter informing me he had nominated a brief and early poem of mine for a Pushcart Prize. The poem, "Epitaph For a Young Man" was written in 1953, and has never appeared in any of my collections. (see page 153) It was a surprise to me when I discovered it a few years ago in one of my numerous files, etc. It is, in fact an unusual poem, and I hope it does win the prize [*Hampden-Sydney Poetry Review*, No. 36, Winter 2010. [Originally published as "Young Man" in *ABZ* poetry magazine, No. 1, 2006]

So, as you see, or hear, it is never too late, and the bum who thinks he has little talent might learn a lesson. Still in my twenties, without a book, when I wrote that short poem, I was just playing with words and verse lines and forms, and no expectations that it might be published and win an award!

So, young fellow, or elder man of verse, just keep reading and learning, and maybe publishing. There are readers out there!

By the way, I liked the photo on your most recent card: the woman and her daughter, working on an old treadle sewing machine. I once owned and used one of those ancient tools: in the homestead years, repairing worn shirts and trousers, maybe a leather mitten or one of my homemade moose-hide moccasins. Not a bad thing back then, and might still be if one needed it and could find one.

Thanks for writing, Rachel, and don't quit on it! The mail is something I need and rely on in these late years. My best wishes to your cats...

 Love,
 John

[ENCLOSED NOTECARD]

Avanti Press
Photo design: Janet Burton

A wide-eyed orange tabby kitten is next to a sleeping beagle whose ear is covering the cat's head.

[John typed:]
Would you please get your big ear-flap
 off my face? Snoose...

              25 Nov-Tanks...

Okay, Rachel, another Cat-Card for you, since you asked for it. And I do mean, please remove that damned ear-flap! I can't sleep well with the smell of it in my nose and the weight of it on my face!

I am enclosing something I would like you to send on for me if you can find their address. I just recently received a copy of the new Ice-Floe issue from the UA Press, and I want to thank the two folks who originated it and are still with it. I know that Shannon and Sarah are there at UAA, and I thought you might find their address and add it to what I have typed on the envelope, already stamped, etc. It was a major surprise to have the new issue in the mail. As a bookstore lady, I'm sure you know of it.

I am otherwise at the moment waiting to be taken to a Tank-giving dinner here. I ain't fond of turkey, but I'm sure there'll also be some sort of roadkill side-dish. Otherwise, I'm gonna have a drink and snooze!

Thanks for the piece on our Ladyship Sarah [Sarah Palin]; I have yet to read all of it. What I've been able to read of Rick Steiner seems to me right on the mark; thanks for sending that also. [Rick Steiner was a marine conservation Professor at University of Alaska from 1980-2010. He is author of *Oasis Earth: Planet in Peril*, Cirque Press, 2020.}

As you know, the weather stuff up here has been a major mess, reminding me of my boyhood winters back east: mush, slick roads, and a damned nuisance. But as a kid I didn't have to drive, and that was a blessing. I slipped and fell yesterday, and left a bad lump on my bone bottom. If you can make it, please come and give me a good rub! Today, things are a bit better, and maybe the ice-arena has shifted south a bit, or moved north to Prudough.

I will keep this note short, as the time is short, and I want to get it in the mail first thing tomorrow...

Love,
John

17 Dec 10

Dear Rachel,

I owe you an apology for waiting so long to respond to yours of Dec 5. But the main factor has been a serious injury I acquired when I slipped and fell in an icy parking lot downtown. My left buttock bone has, for some reason, never recovered, and I have been living with the pain for over two weeks, and with no help in sight. I cannot sit for long (as I am now!), nor do any physical work that involves hip or lower leg, etc. A friend suggested that the injury has developed into something I knew nothing of, but which another physician friend here has more or less confirmed: SCIATICA. Never any experience of this before, though I remember hearing the word when I was young, and my dad spoke of it with one of his male friends.

But I don't want to take up your time with this. I can't go on sitting here to write more to you. I must get up and get this in the mail for you.

Here is the poem you asked for, ["Epitaph for a Young Man"] and I hope it fits whatever occasion you asked for it. Note the date; I was not yet 30, but close to returning to Alaska and the homestead after a long absence.

I'm sorry I haven't better news, but if I cannot find the right help for this affliction I may have to cancel out of the AWP event in February.

Well, dear God, I hope not, but that is what this terrible pain is telling me.

Whatever else, have some good times down there or wherever you may be for the holiday.

Love,
John

EPITAPH FOR A YOUNG MAN

I seemed always standing
before a door
to which I had no key,
although I knew it held behind it
a gift for me.

Until one day I closed
my eyes a moment, stretched,
then looked once more.
And not surprised, I did not mind it
when the hinges creaked
and, smiling, Death held out
his hand to me.

        John Haines
        1953

Correspondence 2011

Jan 10, 2011

Dear Rachel,

Thank you once more for your card and all that you had to say. I did not know your friend, Carol, or not that I can recall meeting her there in your bookstore. I'm sorry you've lost her, and I know what that can be. Two years ago, I was down there in the hospital, as you may know, with a serious case of pneumonia (or was I in hospital here?) These things can be confusing, and I had an additional bout with one thing or another... I can't always recall the subject or the details.

Things here with me are not good, and they seem to be getting worse. I was here alone last night after part of a day dealing with my ailment alone, and things simply got worse as the time went on. I had a good friend, former Montana student from the 1970s; then she had to leave to go back to Anchorage to teach in the coming weeks. So, I was alone, and rather miserable. But I don't want to go into all the details at this time. It is for me a very strange situation, one I would never have expected.

I've been more or less out of touch with everything but this health problem, but I've wanted to add to this card/letter a bit more. I've written no one else, but have had a card or two from friends who are, have been, concerned with me and what I've been dealing with for at least a month now, though it feels to me at times like something I was born with!

But things are, in some respects a bit better, and I hope to wake one day and with the liberation I am due.

I spoke on the phone with my friend Bruce [Guernsey], as to whether or not I'll be able to make it to DC early next month. He's very concerned about this, as I think anyone might understand.

But the clock is ticking, and the time gets on. Another pain appointment in the next hour, and I hope it might have some effect on this new ailment. I can wish for better news to pass on to a dear friend like you, and I'll let you know if in fact this might be true. I have a good man friend who will come to pick me up and take me to the Med Center; without his help I might not make it.

So, dear Rachel, I very much regret all of this and at this special time. I'll let you know the outcome (when it comes!). At least the subzero has given us a break, and I'm glad for that. I hope to have better news for you in a future card.

Love, and my best to you…

John

[ENCLOSED NOTECARD]

Pomegranate Communications, Inc.

Red Squirrel, 1578

Hans Hoffmann (German, c. 1545/1550-1591/1592, National Gallery of Art, Washington, DC)

Words, Writings, and Letters

23 Jan 11

Dear Rachel,

    I have your Jan 13 card, one of the best you have sent me, and to know that you continue [to] care about this old bard, stricken as he is at this time. Things are not much better, but I can at least type and see the result on the page (or card). I cannot recall what I might have told you, but I spent two nights in the local hospital and emerged exhausted, nothing serene.

    However, I have made a decision to go to... DC in Feb., for the AWP event. I hope to be in shape for that, hardly a week away. I had thought to skip on it, unable to make the passage, but I know now how much it means to Bruce [Guernsey], Steve [Rogers], and others, and I don't want to disappoint them. If, on the other hand, something occurs to make it impossible…, Well, I know folks will understand and be able to accept the painful truth of things. If I do make it, I hope to see you there with my Wheelchair ready!

I could write more, Lady Epstein, and I may, but wanted to get this much in the mail to you ere the time runs out. I would sure love to have some crunchy nuts or seeds to munch on! We bushy folks in the trees, etc., need a bite when we can get it!

Love, as always…

John

JOHN MEADE HAINES

JUNE 29, 1924 - MARCH 2, 2011

There was no further response to my next letters. All was quiet from Fairbanks.

❧

I learned about John Haines' death from an email sent by Steve Rogers. The obituaries published by various newspapers—the *New York Times, Anchorage Daily News, Fairbanks Daily News-Miner*—printed much of the same narrative: John Haines chose poetry because his paints froze at Richardson; his first book of poems, *Winter News,* brought him national recognition and acclaim; he was known to have had a notorious cantankerous disposition as well as five failed marriages; throughout his life, he had no reliable employment or secure academic position.

John Haines' close friend, John Kooistra, sent me a copy of the memorial service that was planned in Fairbanks. After one phone conversation, we no longer communicated.

PART II.

Life Between Poetry and Place

DISCORD AND DISSONANCE, ENDING THOUGHTS

Compiling John Meade Haines' words, writings, and letters from 2009-2011 brings together a variety of feelings. It was unusual how our friendship developed through the exchange of letters. We shared a hunger for critical historical discourse and a natural love of literature. Our stars crossed for two years and his laughter and curious intellect are gifts he left me. Others knew John Haines in different settings. Many unfamiliar to me.

For many Alaskans, the poems "Winter News," "Poem of the Forgotten," "Fairbanks Under the Solstice," "Little Cosmic Dust Poem," "Return to Richardson, Spring 1981", and "A Requiem for the Arctic Refuge" spring to mind when remembering him.

In another manner, literary scholars concerned with John Meade Haines' place in the American literary tradition debate the application of regional, nature, political, and eco-poetry labels.

That Alaska cultivated John Meade Haines' identity as a poet, writer and activist should not be overshadowed. However, living with many disappointments, John Haines often returned to Alaska searching for connection, academic position, and Alaska friends. His travels from place to place, teaching as a visiting lecturer at various universities, acquiring writing fellowships and short-term residencies for support created both distance and an attachment to Alaska. Keeping his past, present, and tenuous future aligned became increasingly strenuous. Ultimately, he wanted no earthly home for his body, no grave or marker at Richardson, the place that changed his life forever.

Going beyond personal introspection and literary assessments, it will be for future readers to discover John Meade Haines and his timely relevance. My hope is that John Haines will not fade from collective memory but will continue to influence, inspire, and nurture creative expression within and beyond Alaska.

IF THE OWL CALLS AGAIN

at dusk
from the island in the river,
and it's not too cold,

I'll wait for the moon
to rise,
then take wing and glide
to meet him.

We will not speak,
but hooded against the frost
soar above
the alder flats, searching
with tawny eyes.

And then we'll sit
in the shadowy spruce
and pick the bones
of careless mice,

while the long moon drifts
toward Asia
and the river mutters
in its icy bed.

And when the morning climbs
the limbs
we'll part without a sound,

fulfilled, floating
homeward as
the cold world awakens.

"If the Owl Calls Again"—the first poem in John Haines' first poetry collection, *Winter News*—sets the imaginative and escapist tone heard in many of John Haines' later poems.

ॐ

An Afternoon at John Haines' Homestead, Richardson, Alaska, October 2011

Photographs by Ray Bonnell, author of "Sketches of Alaska"

Tanana River Valley – "from the island in the river"

John Haines' cabin at Richardson

Life Between Poetry and Place

Bench on top of ridge

FIVE POEMS AND AN ESSAY

The following poems represent John Haines' finest work in their literary strength and beauty. They encompass themes of love, hope, friendship, and place. The poems are filled with intimate reflections, graced to expand the mind and emit feeling. The essay expresses the importance and need for artists. And it describes the fundamental relationship between nature, artists, and art.

    150   "Rain Country"
    156   "In the Forest Without Leaves XV"
    158   "The Ice Child"
    160   "Fourth of July at Santa Ynez"
    162   "The Snowbound City"
    163   "The Creative Spirit in Art and Literature," essay

RAIN COUNTRY

Earth. Nothing more.
Earth. Nothing less.
And let that be enough for you.

—Pedro Salinas (1891-1951, Spanish poet
and member of Generation '27)

I

The woods are sodden,
and the last leaves
tarnish and fall.

Thirty-one years ago
this rainy autumn
we walked home from the lake,
Campbell and Peg and I,
over the shrouded dome,
the Delta wind in our faces,
home through the drenched
and yellowing woodland.

Bone-chilled but with singing
hearts we struck our fire
from the stripped bark
and dry, shaven aspen;
and while the stove-iron
murmured and cracked
and our wet wool steamed,
we crossed again

the fire-kill of timber
in the saddle of Deadwood—

down the windfall slope,
by alder thicket, and now
by voice alone, to drink
from the lake at evening.

A mile and seven days
beyond the grayling pool
at Deep Creek, the promised
hunt told of a steepness
in the coming dusk.

II

Light in the aspen wood
on Campbell's hill,
a fog trail clearing below,
as evenly the fall distance
stretched the summer sun.

Our faces strayed together
in the cold north window—
night, and the late cup
steaming before us...
Campbell, his passion
tamed by the tumbling years,
an old voice retelling.

As if a wind has stopped us
listening on the trail,
we turned to a sound
the earth made that morning—

a heavy rumble in the gray
hills toward Fairbanks;
our mountain shivered
underfoot, and all
the birds were still.

   III

Shadows blur in the rain,
they are whispering straw
and talking leaves.

I see what does not exist,
hear voices that cannot speak
through the packed
earth that fills them.

Loma, in the third year
of war, firing at night
from his pillow
for someone to waken.

Campbell, drawing a noose
in the dust at his feet:
"Creation was seven days,
no more, no less..."
Noah and the flooded earth
were clouded in his mind.

And Knute, who turned
from his radio one August
afternoon, impassioned
and astonished:

                    "Is that
the government? I ask you—
is *that* the government?"

Bitter Melvin, who nailed
his warning above the doorway:

Please don't shoot
the beevers
They are my friends.

   IV

And all the stammering folly
aimed toward us
from the rigged pavilions—
malign dictations, insane
pride of the fox-eyed men
who align the earth
to a tax-bitten dream
of metal and smoke—

all drank of the silence
to which we turned:
one more yoke at the spring,
another birch rick balanced,
chilled odor and touch
of the killed meat quartered
and racked in the shade.

It was thirty-one years ago
this rainy autumn.

Of the fire we built to warm us,
and the singing heart
driven to darkness
on the time-bitten-earth—

only a forest rumor
whispers through broken straw
and trodden leaves
how late in a far summer
three friends came home,
walking the soaked ground
of an ancient love.

   V

Much rain has fallen. Fog
drifts in the spruce boughs,
heavy with alder smoke,
denser than I remember.

Campbell is gone, in an old age
struck down one early winter;
and Peg in her slim youth
long since become a stranger.
The high, round hill of Buckeye
stands whitened and cold.

I am not old, not yet, though
like a wind-turned birch
spared by the axe,
I claim this clearing
in the one country I know.

Remembering, fitting names
to a rain-soaked map:
Gold Run, Minton, Tenderfoot,
McCoy. Here Melvin killed
his grizzly, there Wilkins
built his forge. All
that we knew, and everything
but for me forgotten.

VI

I write this down
in the brown ink of leaves,
of the changed pastoral
deepening to mist on my page.

I see in the shadow-pool
beneath my hand a mile
and thirty years beyond
this rain-driven autumn.

All that we loved: a fire
long dampened, the quenched
whispering down of faded
straw and yellowing leaves.

The names, and the voices
within them, speak now
for the slow rust of things
that are muttered in sleep.

There is ice on the water
I look through, the steep
rain turning to snow.

IN THE FOREST WITHOUT LEAVES XV

...Believe me, he alone
is interesting who still
loves something.
 —Jacob Burckhardt (1818-1897, Swiss Historian)

In the forest without leaves
stands a birch tree,
slender and white.

For the sun drank pallor
from its leaves,
and the marrow in its roots
froze down.

Only the paper bark stayed
to weather and peel,
be sunlight or tinder
burned in the hunter's fire,

and wind took away all the rest.

If and whenever we come again,
I will know that tree.

A birch leaf held fast
in limestone ten million years
still quietly burns,
though claimed by the darkness.

Let earth be this windfall
swept to a handful of seeds—
one tree, one leaf,
gives us plenty of light.

THE ICE CHILD

Cold for so long, unable to speak,
yet your mouth seems framed
on a cry, or a stifled question.

Who placed you here, and left you
to this lonely eternity of ash and ice,
and himself returned to the dust
fields, the church and the temple?

Was it God—the sun-god of the Incas,
the imperial god of the Spaniards?
Or only the priests of that god,
self-elected—voice of the volcano
that speaks once in a hundred years.

And I wonder, with your image before me,
what life might you have lived,
had you lived at all—whose companion,
whose love? To be perhaps no more
than a slave of that earthly master:

a jug of water on your shoulder,
year after stunted year, a bundle
of reeds and corn, kindling
for a fire on whose buried hearth?

There were furies to be fed, then
as now: blood to fatten the sun,
a heart for the lightning to strike.

And now the furies walk the streets,
a swarm in the milling crowd.
They stand to the podium, speak
of their coming ascension...

Through all this drift and clamor
you have survived—in this cramped
and haunted effigy, another entry
on the historian's dated page.

Under the weight of this mountain—
once a god, now only restless stone,
we find your interrupted life,
placed here among the trilobites
and shells, so late unearthed.

FOURTH OF JULY AT SANTA YNEZ

I

Under the makeshift arbor of leaves
a hot wind blowing smoke and laughter.
Music out of the renegade west,
too harsh and loud, many dark faces
moved among the sweating whites.

II

Wandering apart from the others,
I found an old Indian seated alone
on a bench in the flickering shade.

He was holding a dented bucket;
three crayfish, lifting themselves
from the muddy water, stirred
scrapped against the greasy metal.

III

The old man stared from his wrinkled
darkness across the celebration,
unblinking, as one might see
in the hooded sleep of turtles.

A smile out of the ages of gold
and carbon flashed upon his face
and vanished, called away
by the sound and the glare around him,
by the lost voice of a child
piercing that thronged solitude.

IV

The afternoon gathered distance
and depth, divided in the shadows
that broke and moved upon us...

Slowly, too slowly, as if returned
from a long and difficult journey,
the old man lifted his bucket
and walked away into the sunlit crowd.

THE SNOWBOUND CITY

I believe in this stalled magnificence,
this churning chaos of traffic,
a beast with broken spine,
its hoarse voice hooded in feathers
and mist; the baffled eyes
wink amber and slowly darken.

Of men and women suddenly walking,
stumbling with little sleighs
in search of Tibetan houses—
dust from a far-off mountain
already whitens their shoulders.

When evening falls in blurred heaps,
a man losing his way among churches
and schoolyards feels under his cold hand
the stone thoughts of that city,

impassable to all but a few children
who went on into the hidden life
of caves and winter fires,
their faces glowing with disaster.

THE CREATIVE SPIRIT IN ART AND LITERATURE
(from *Fables and Distances: New and Selected Essays*)

In the movement of trees,
I find my own agitation...

> —Wallace Stevens (1879-1955)
> from *Opus Posthumous*

Three years ago, while at home in Alaska, I was sitting at the desk in my small study in the woods one early summer morning, and looking out the window at a birch tree just beginning to bud. The dark branches mounting at intervals up the trunk were in sharp contrast to the pale, papery bark. It was a scene I had watched many times in the past. And as I was watching, I saw a bird, a warbler, flitting from branch to branch, from twig to twig, up and down the tree in search of insects. The image of that bird in relation to the tree and its branches was arresting—in its constant, flitting movements, and then in its sudden significance. For it struck me that here, in a single and astonishing impression, might be seen an early stage of musical notation, with the bars and notes ascending and descending in scale.

For many years I made the better part of my living from the wilderness of the Far North, in Alaska. That is, I hunted and fished, gathered food from the countryside. In doing this over a period of many years I learned, in what I think a true sense, to *read* and interpret the country: the ground underfoot, the coming and going of creatures, the arrival and departure of birds, the seasonal flowering and fading of plant life. These things, the physical evidence of them, constitute a language, a grammar, and a syntax; they represent in some way the original perception we may have acquired of a fundamental order in things, in their relationships and significant connections. And I mean by this, among other things, story, narrative, the thread of sequence and consequence.

There is a close connection between reading signs in the snow—the imprint of a bird's wing, or the scattering of leaves and seeds over the surface—and reading words on a page; the same inherent order and process is at work in both of these. And as the spring sun erases the snow and all of its signs and evidence, so do we from time to time find it necessary to erase what we have written and begin over, for the sake of a clearer definition and understanding.

The secret of creativity, of creative imagination, is not to be discovered in a laboratory, nor in abstract theory, nor in any dissection of the brain or the nervous system, nor in computer models of *intelligence*—thinking machines and mechanical pseudopods—but in attention to the world, and for me that means primarily attention to the natural world, to such vital relationships as we may perceive there.

For when we begin looking—and I mean really looking, with an attention cleared of formulations and preconceptions—we begin to see combinations and possibilities, order and beauty, anywhere. Walking, seeing the reflections of trees in standing pools, the light of the sun on leaves and water; the shapes of buildings and houses, the textures of stonework and pavement, the movement of clouds over the landscape: here, under our feet and close at hand, can be found those primary patterns of creative order...

...The ordering, the unifying or harmonizing, of scattered and apparently unrelated material is the very essence of the creative impulse. And this activity is everywhere much the same, whether it means ordering the characters and events in a story, the placing of objects and figures upon the ground of a painting, the arranging of objects in a room to make a pleasing and habitable space, or the placing of certain words and sequences of words in a metrical structure we call verse, or in a paragraphic order we know as prose. And one would have to say, too, that this basic description applies to systems of thought, as well as to political and economic systems of social and hierarchical order.

Life Between Poetry and Place

This is what I understand as the creative process. What we refer to as artistic vision is an ability on the part of some individuals—poets, artists, and thinkers—to grasp and present to us in visible form a kind of totality of relationships, which represents in some way the greater totality of existence...

⁂

These photos, taken over 3 decades, present John Haines in his literary habitat with poets, friends, and colleagues.

Wendell Berry and John Haines, Portland, Oregon, 1982 *(William Stafford Collection: Stafford Photo Exhibit 2014, #68; photograph by William Stafford, reprinted by permission of the Estate of William Stafford)*

1990 Alaskan Poetry Festival in Fairbanks Left to right: Christianne Balk, Tom Sexton, Robert Hoffmann Davis, John Haines, Nora Marks Dauenhauer, John Morgan, William Wadsworth *(Photo credit: Peggy Shumaker)*

At the time of the 1990 Poetry Festival: **Christianne Balk** is author of the poetry collection *Bindweed* (1986) and is recipient of the 1985 Walt Whitman Award. **Tom Sexton** earned a Master of Fine Arts degree from University of Alaska (Fairbanks) and went on to establish the English Department at the University of Alaska Anchorage where he began teaching in 1970. **Robert Hoffmann Davis** belongs to the Tlingit tribe Eagle/Killer Whale clan, Yellow Cedar House and is from Kake, Alaska. A highly renowned wood carver, painter, and poet, his first book of poetry, *SoulCatcher*, was published in 1986. Existential life with metaphysical Raven is explored in many of his poems. **John Haines** is the author of nationally acclaimed collections of poetry including *Winter News* (1966), *The Stone Harp* (1970), *News from the Glacier: Selected Poems 1960-1980* (1982). His book *New Poems 1980-1988* (1990) received the Lenore Marshall Poetry Prize and the Western States Book Award. **Nora Marks Dauenhauer** belongs to the Tlingit tribe Raven/Sockeye clan, Canoe

Prow House situated on the Alsek River. A highly revered culture bearer, linguist, and poet, she is author of *Haa Shuká, Our Ancestors: Tlingit Oral Narratives* (1987); *The Droning Shaman: Poems* (English and Tlingit Edition) (1989); *Haa Tuwunáagu Yís, for Healing Our Spirit: Tlingit Oratory* (1990). **John Morgan** came to Fairbanks in 1976 to direct the Creative Writing program at the University of Alaska (Fairbanks). He studied under poet Robert Lowell at Harvard University and is author of the poetry collection *Arctic Herd* (1984). **William Wadsworth** is the recent Academy of American Poets executive director.

John Haines and Tom Sexton, Anchorage, Alaska, 2009 *(Photo credit: Lila Vogt)*

AN OVERVIEW OF CONTRASTS: JOHN HAINES' LIFE BETWEEN POETRY AND PLACE

This overview of contrasts encompassing John Haines' life, work, and achievements is crafted to promote discourse and further understanding of his literary career. It can be a guide to accompany this book or, in addition, serve to provide navigation points for further assessment of his contributions to American literature.

1. The miners near Richardson were John Haines' friends and mentors who taught him how to survive on the land. Their uncommon virtues were referred to in many of his poems and essays. During the Alaska Writer Laureates' event John stated that he had recently discovered that the men burned the forest to acquire dry, dead wood for kindling. He stated he wished they had not done that. "It's a mixed business." This surprising realization became an unsettling fact that John had to contend with even though it came late in his life.

2. Although John Haines held consistent antiwar convictions, he greatly admired his father, a Navy Admiral, who received the Navy Cross for valor and is buried in Arlington National Cemetery. One of Haines' favorite poets was Jorge Manrique whose gallant verses advocated living a glorified life, one that ended in battle. John often recited or sang Manrique stanzas in Spanish to whomever was around and to whomever would listen: at the USA Artist gathering and during a stay in the Fairbanks hospital. In a contrary manner, his blunt antiwar poem "Arlington" (published in 1977) can be considered a classic of that genre. In the essay "Wartime: A Late Memoir," we find another, more reflective, John Haines. First published in 2004 in the *Sewanee*

Review and later published in *Descent*, John Haines addressed the complexities of his wartime experiences on the *USS Knapp* (DD-653) and the lessons there that he found:

> Things were growing more and more serious out in the battle zone, and our ship and crew as well as others now returning from the West Coast were urgently needed. Our arrival at Okinawa occurred in the midst of one of the worst battles of the Pacific war. We sailed into a harbor on the main island to see so many damaged and half-sunken ships, some of which were upended in the dark evening water of the harbor. It was, as I remarked at the time, like entering a graveyard, made all the more devastating because several of the badly damaged or sunken ships had accompanied us in previous engagements.
>
> Our destroyers were placed on picket duty, patrolling the coastline and the waters outside the island. We were to intercept the suicide planes that flew down nightly from Japan to plunge into and destroy any American vessel they encountered. Our nights were nearly sleepless. All was in darkness aboard ship; our eyes were focused on the flashes and signals of the radar screen and, when possible, on what could be seen of land and horizon in the darkness. It was a ghostly, almost surreal period in its nighttime silence, its inherent mystery and uncertainty. Only once were we directly menaced when, in what was then daylight, one of the suicide bombers, perhaps damaged by aircraft fire, soared over our ship and plunged into the sea. It was close, and many ships of our fleet were not so lucky…
>
> …In thinking about that war and my own experience of it, I have come to feel that there is at least one important lesson to be learned: that there are certain things about oneself, one's character, and about humanity in general, that one may never know until one has been, if only for a brief time, in mortal danger—at extreme risk, physically and psychologically, and in which one's

very existence is in doubt. There are no rules for this, and for the individual at times it may very well prove otherwise than I have stated here. But in that situation of mortal risk there can be a momentary focus of energy and attention, the like of which might for some be found in intellectual life, and which I feel to be, in certain important respects, a fundamental fact of our earthly life.

At times, it can be difficult to choose between John Haines the philosopher and John Haines the poet. Both are profoundly serious and whole.

3. There is a romantic mystique surrounding John Haines that by existing in an untamed environment he had little contact with people or literary influences outside of Alaska. At the Alaska Writer Laureates' panel, he credited Li Po and other classical Chinese masters for inspiring his early poetry and style. William Butler Yeats, Wallace Stevens, Miguel Hernandez, and many other poets can be heard in John Haines' poetry. The romantic poem "Harvest" was inspired by the poem "Erntezeit" by Friedrich Hölderlin (1770-1843). The poem "The Glutton" was inspired by the painting "The Seven Deadly Sins" attributed to Hieronymus Bosch (1450-1516).

Greed, Scene from the Table of the Seven Deadly Sins *(Photo credit: Hieronymus Bosch—Greed, Scene from the Table of the Seven Deadly Sins, c.1480, courtesy of www.hieronymus-bosch.org)*

THE GLUTTON

Another drumstick, dear wife,
another tun of beer!
And please do not forget
the pudding—
put in another plum!

Oh! I am so round and button—
snapping, so tuckered
with fat and swill—
And yet, and yet...
I think there is room for more!

Let the bailiff come rudely
Knocking...I will dream
of a great, slotted spoon,
of a bowl as deep as a tub
to hold and to rock me;

and no one unkindly to mention
how I roll and snort
through the night—until,
set down at the kitchen
door, I am ready
already for breakfast.

All would be well, my dearest—
the cupboard crammed
with bacon, with sweating hams
and fat yellow cheeses,
the counter board dripping
with tripe and lights;

and over the table and over
the floor, litter of larks
and sparrows, crumbs
of cake and clots of cream...

All would be well, and all
forgiven, were it not
for this brat I have fathered,
who looks all too much
like me, and would eat more
than I—

> Tucked so tightly
> into his chair, who beats
> his bowl with a spoon,
> crying:
> > Feed me! Feed me!

4. Although he had not earned degrees in higher education, John Haines was a recipient of numerous prestigious awards including the Lenore Marshall Poetry Prize, an Alaska Governor's Award for Excellence in the Arts, the Poets' Prize, a Lifetime Achievement Award from the Library of Congress, and the Aitken Taylor Award for Modern American Poetry.

5. John Haines' relationship to those teaching at the University of Alaska and to those associated with academia in general was one of conflict. That he was not given the sufficient respect he merited is a fact. In his Dryden/Pope inspired poem "UA Dunciad," John Haines skillfully condemned the administration and individual faculty members at the University of Alaska Fairbanks. Written in 1998, John was so proud of his accomplishment that for years he openly shared it with friends while enjoying many good laughs. It was his way of seeking poetic revenge.

6. While nearing the end of his life at age 86, the annual Association of Writers & Writing Programs (AWP)—something John Haines had not associated himself with—featured a session dedicated to John Meade Haines. Many academic figures and friends of John participated in the tribute. Regrettably, due to his deteriorating health, John was unable to attend the February 2011 event. From the letters, one can see how much the gathering meant to him.

7. Leaving Alaska was a theme referred to in many of John Haines' writings. That he should never have left was a repeated refrain. Yet, many of his exceptional poems were written outside of Alaska, i.e., "Rain Country," "Night," and "On a Certain Field in Auvers," about the painter Van Gogh.

8. It could be claimed that leaving Alaska was an unfaithful act, a type of abandonment of Richardson, Fairbanks, and the Alaskan community. John Haines' collection *Winter News* was remarkable because people living close to the tundra could identify with the poems—the images, language, and sensations that stem from survival in the north—poems that enhanced everyday life for those who ventured to Alaska and stayed. *Winter News* connected people with Alaska in a way that no other book had. Reviewers in the lower 48 described its surreal quality; yet the collection was quite grounded in Alaska and the magnetic north. "They say the wells are freezing at Northway where the cold begins," was not poetic license or imagination but something real that people in Alaska related to.

9. It appears that leaving Alaska was not simply a repeated mistake. In the poem "Missoula in a Dusty Light," John Haines granted Missoula an intimacy comparable to Fairbanks, both in description and language.

MISSOULA IN A DUSTY LIGHT

Walking home through the tall
Montana twilight,
leaves were moving in the gutters
and a little dust...

I saw beyond the roofs and chimneys
a cloud like a hill of smoke,
amber and a dirty gray. And a wind

began from the street corners
and rutted alleys,
out of year-end gardens, weed lots
and trash bins;
              the yellow air
came full of specks and ash,
noiseless, crippled things that crashed
and flew again...
grit and the smell of rain.

And then a steady sound,
as if an army or a council,
long-skirted, sweeping the stone,
were gathering near;
disinherited and vengeful people,
scuffing their bootheels,
rolling tin cans before them.

And quieter still behind them
the voices of birds
and whispering brooms:
                    "This land
has bitter roots, and seeds
that crack and spill in the wind..."

I halted under a blowing light
to listen, to see;
and it was the bleak Montana wind
sweeping the leaves and dust
along the street.

10. When living in Montana, John Haines separated from his wife Joy DeStefano for a variety of reasons; however, the lack of income factored into it. At the Alaska Writer Laureates' panel, when asked why he was in Alaska he replied he had no other place to go.

11. There are many people in Fairbanks who had known John Haines informally, over decades, who said they had not been aware of John's grim living situation. Two close friends mentioned that the problem was "John had no family."

12. In my view, one of John Haines' finest poems is "To Vera Thompson." In it he changes places with Vera Thompson, the woman whose headstone stands before him in the Eagle cemetery in Alaska. When reading the poem, many people experience visualizing themselves in John Haines' place. Defiantly, though, John Haines did not want a marker posted at Richardson after he died. That unsettling decision begs one to pause, take a moment, and ask the question, why?

TO VERA THOMPSON

(Buried in the Old Military Cemetery at Eagle, Alaska)

Woman whose face
is a blurred map of roots,
I might be buried here
and you dreaming in the warmth
of this late northern summer.

Say I was the last
soldier on the Yukon,
my war fought out
with leaves and thorns.

Here is the field;
it lies thick with horsetail,
fireweed, and stubborn rose.
The wagons and stables
followed the troopers
deep into soil and smoke.
When a summer visitor
steps over the rotting sill
the barracks floor
thumps with a hollow sound.

Life and death grow quieter
and lonelier here by the river.
Summer and winter
the town sleeps and settles,
history is no more than sunlight
on a weathered cross.

The picket fence sinks
to a row of mossy shadows,
the gate locks with a rusty pin.
Stand there now
and say that you loved me,
that I will not be forgotten
when a ghostwind
drifts through the canyon,
and our years grow deep
under snow of these roses and stones.

13. Although the people closest to John Haines maintain they had done the best they could for the Alaska "man of letters," a cold rush comes over me when I revisit the obituaries published days after his death.

John Haines "found inspiration in the peaks of the Alaskan range that he could see from the cabin he built himself, in the butterfly he held in his hands, in the moose he shot and butchered. He told of stones waiting for God to remember their names... [His] memoir, "The Stars, the Snow, the Fire" (1989), told of the first fox he killed by hand, and of making dog food from a porcupine... A reviewer noted that he revealed more about his sled dogs than he did about his wives." (From "John Haines, a Poet of the Wild, Dies at 86", *New York Times*, March 5, 2011, by Douglass Martin.)

"Haines sold his homestead in 1969 and began a checkered life of travel, relocations, and relationships... Living some miles from town, off Farmer's Loop Road, he seemed particularly upset by the inconvenience of depending on others for transportation... On February 24, [John] Kooistra was called to Haines' house... but Haines did not want to go to the hospital again. Kooistra discovered his old friend dehydrated and undernourished. "We loaded him in a chair and I drove him to the emergency room," Kooistra recounted. "Haines said, 'Well, I'll go for a day. I've got too much to do.'" (From "Former state poet laureate, homesteader and Alaska literary lion John Haines died Wednesday in Fairbanks. He was 86," *Anchorage Daily News*, March 3, 2011, by Mike Dunham.)

14. In *The Owl in the Mask of the Dreamer: Collected Poems,* Part II Notes, John Haines offered this definition of his poetry: "... All of the poems bear witness to my attempts to discover a language and poetic means of my own, and relate my experience as wilderness inhabitant and literate man to a tradition, ancient or modern."

So to you the reader, I ask, who was John Meade Haines, and did he fulfill his quest as poet?

A SUN, DISTANT WITHIN: ELEVEN POEMS AND AN ESSAY

The following poems and essay are for those curious about the writings mentioned in *May the Owl Call Again: A Return to Poet John Meade Haines, 1924-2011*. They highlight and expose a nonlinear progression of thought that can be found in John Haines' oeuvre. The sections also categorize John Haines' immediate, external, and internal environments: of senses, mind, and heart.

Solitary Life and Nature

- "Poem of the Forgotten"
  (in Discord and Dissonance, Ending Thoughts)
- "Tenderfoot"
  (referred to in a letter)
- "Fairbanks Under the Solstice"
  (in Discord and Dissonance, Ending Thoughts)

Romantic Love and Passion

- "Harvest"
  (referred to in a letter)
- "Little Cosmic Dust Poem"
  (in Discord and Dissonance, Ending Thoughts)
- "Return to Richardson, Spring 1981"
  (in Discord and Dissonance, Ending Thoughts)

Truth and Poetic Conscience:

- "Shadows II"
  (essay referred to in a letter)
- "A Requiem for the Arctic Refuge"
  (in Discord and Dissonance, Ending Thoughts)
- "Night"
  (referred to in a letter)
- "Arlington"
  (in An Overview of Contrasts: John Haines' Life Between Poetry and Place)

Death and The Light Within:

- "On a Certain Field in Auvers"
  (in Overview of Contrasts: John Haines' Life Between Poetry and Place)
- "Meditation on a Skull Carved in Crystal'
  (the last poem featured in the book)

POEM OF THE FORGOTTEN

I came to this place,
a young man green and lonely.

Well quit of the world,
I framed a house of moss and timber,
called it home,
and sat in the warm evenings
singing to myself as a man sings
when he knows there is no one to hear.

I made my bed under the shadow
of leaves, and awoke
in the first snow of autumn,
filled with silence.

TENDERFOOT

It is dusk back there, the road
is empty and the log house quiet.

Jessie, the Indian girl, stands
at the doorway in silence,
her thin face turned to the earth.

No more than an aching shadow,
her father bends at the sawhorse,
cutting the last dry pole.

The swallow box has fallen,
the catalogue had lost its pages.

The black mouths of the rain barrels
are telling of migrations,
the whispering rush
of a lonely people toward the past.

FAIRBANKS UNDER THE SOLSTICE

Slowly, without sun, the day sinks
toward the close of December.
It is minus sixty degrees.

Over the sleeping houses a dense
fog rises—smoke from banked fires,
and the snowy breath of an abyss
through which the cold town
is perceptively falling.

As if Death were a voice made visible,
with the power of illumination...

Now, in the white shadow
of those streets, ghostly newsboys
make their rounds, delivering
to the homes of those
who have died of the frost
word of the resurrection of Silence.

HARVEST

There will be much to remember,
a load of wood
on your shoulders, a dusty
sack in your arms, full
of the smell of rutabagas
and winter cabbage.

For the paths are rough,
and the days come on
like driven horses.

But we have kept faith
with ourselves.

We will not look back
but press on, deeper
than the source of water,
to the straw-filled cave
of beginnings.

There in the vegetable darkness
to strike a match, kindling
the cold, untraveled sun.

LITTLE COSMIC DUST POEM

Out of the debris of dying stars,
this rain of particles
that waters the waste with brightness...

The sea-wave of atoms hurrying home,
collapse of the giant,
unstable guest who cannot stay...

The sun's heart reddens and expands,
his mighty aspiration is lasting,
as the shell of his substance
one day will be white with frost.

In the radiant field of Orion
great hordes of stars are forming,
just as we see every night,
fiery and faithful to the end.

Out of the cold and fleeing dust
that is never and always,
the silence and waste to come...

This arm, this hand,
my voice, your face, this love.

RETURN TO RICHARDSON, SPRING 1981

Somber now, the grizzly hills,
the lake water slack and gray
between the shore and candle ice.

I walk a path under birch and aspen
still leafless in this early April.
Another winter, old neighbors long
departed, and the pole bridge fallen.
I see underfoot, black in the rusty
soil, the leaves of a lost summer.

*

I remember: it was my hand on the axe
that cleared the trees from this path;
that turned and fenced the garden,
the same hand that split and piled
the cordwood, far back in a time
of grace between the Asian wars.

And I remember the two of us then,
after a long day's work in the hills,
quiet with a book between us, the lamp
turned, the title long forgotten.

Those words, read late in the evening,
the pages turned by this hand.
Your voice as you turned to sleep,
and our life like a boat set loose,
going down in the lighted dusk.

*

It is one more spring in the north.
Over the snow-patched land
a brown wind drives a late flurry
down from the granite ranges.

In this restless air I know,
on this ground I can never forget,
where will I set my foot
with so much passion again.

SHADOWS II

(from *We Make A Fire, Orca Anthology of Poems and Prose,* 1982, edited by Cheryl Morse)

There are shadows over the land. They come out of the ground, from the dust and the tumbled bones of the earth; they people the air around us in the shapes of leaves and flying things. Tree shadows that haunt the woodlands and childhood, holding fear in their branches. Stone shadows on the desert, cloud shadows on the sea and over the summer hills, bringing water. Shapes of shadows in pools and wells, vague forms in the sand light.

Out of the past come these wind-figures, the flapping sails of primitive birds with terrible beaks and claws. Shadows of things that walked once and went away. Lickers of blood that fasten by night to the veins of standing cattle, to the foot of a sleeping man. In the far north, the heavy, stalled bodies of mastodons chilled in a black ooze, and their fur-clad bones still come out of the ground. Triceratops was feeding in the marshlands, by the verge of the coal-making forest.

Shadows in the doorways, and under the eaves of ancient buildings, where the fallen creatures of stone grimace in sleep. Domestic, wind-tugged shadows cast by icy branches upon a bedroom window: they tap on the glass and wake us. They speak to the shadows within us, old ghosts that will not die. Like trapped, primordial birds they break from an ice-pool in the heart's well and fly into walls built long ago.

Stand still where you are—at the end of pavement, in a sun break of the forest, on the open, cloud-peopled terrace of the plains. Look deeply into the wind-furrows of the grass, into the leaf-stilled water of pools. Think back through the silence, of the life that was and is not here now, of the strong pastness of things—shadows of the end and the beginning.

It is autumn. Leaves are flying, a storm of them over the land. They are brown and yellow, parched and pale—Shelley's "pestilence-stricken multitudes." Out of an evening darkness they fly in our faces and scare us; like resigned spirits they whirl away and spill into hollows, to lie still, one on the other, waiting for snow.

I stepped out into the yard on a warm October evening, just before dark. I forget now why I had gone out—perhaps for an armload of wood, or to check on the last of the sunset and the oncoming night sky. In those days, when I was done with eating and sleeping, the natural place for me to be was outdoors.

I hadn't been out long when I saw what I at first thought was a large, dark leaf blowing toward me in the dusk; but there was no wind. Like a silent and tumbling leaf it brushed by me and disappeared behind the house. Moments later it returned, darting erratically overhead, and again it dropped from sight, this time down the road toward the river. It occurred to me that it might be a late swallow, but it seemed too dark, silent and strange, and so far as I knew all swallows had long since left the country.

Again the strange visitor fluttered past me in the semi-darkness. And I suddenly knew that this swift, wayward, climbing and falling thing was a bat, that there was more than one of them in the dusk around me. I went to the house door and called to my wife to come and see them. In the warm fall twilight that was slowly waging into night, we both stood and watched.

It was impossible to keep track of them in that dim light. As soon as we had one fixed in flight against the sky, it flew down into the darkness of the trees and vanished. They flew with a queer, jerky movement—a flight somewhat like that of a butterfly, but stronger and swifter. It was as if in that stillness in which they flew a sudden and unfelt gust of wind snatched them aside; or that at any moment they reached the limit of an invisible string that yanked them from their path.

We knew nothing about bats. Never before had one of them come to the yard, and never in many evening walks to the river had I seen one near the water. We had only their swift flight in the dusk around us, the mysteriousness of their appearance in a country from which all other summer creatures had gone. In a kind of spell we watched them for as long as we could distinguish any movement into the darkness. The fall night closed over the landscape, leaving a few stray gleams of light on the river, and we went back indoors.

Looking among the nature guides on our shelf, I found a section on bats and began reading. I learned that the earliest fossil bat has been dated back to the Eocene, ninety-five million years after the first bird flapped through the Jurassic skies, and long after the last flying reptile had become part of the earth's stone history. The teeth and skulls of fossil bats were similar to those of early monkeys, suggesting a common ancestor. And the writer went on to say that bats may be our earliest relatives in the non-monkey world.

Only two kinds of bats were to be found in the Far North, and in Alaska these were said to be limited to an area two or three hundred miles to the south of us. I soon decided, from my reading and from what I had been able to observe of their size and flight habits, that our bats were the *Little Brown Myotis*, one of the smallest and commonest of North American bats. They belonged to a widespread family of insect-feeding bats, having a body no larger than that of a meadow mouse, and with a wingspread of perhaps ten inches. I read that they were colonial in their habits, that some individuals hibernated during the winter, while others migrated; that they slept by day in caves, in old buildings and hollow trees; in deep dusk they could be seen flying near water or at the edge of the forest. And what I was reading seemed to be true, for here they were, hunting our cleared spaces among the birch trees.

The next evening I walked up the highway to our mailbox to post a letter. Again the evening was still and warm, with an occasional light air moving over the hills and a warm light gleaming on the river channel in the southwest. I soon saw a bat flying up and down the roadway, back and forth, swiftly changing altitude in pursuit of the insects that were still abroad. More than once it vanished at the limit of the trees bordering the roadside, to reappear as a leaf-shaped thing against the clear night sky. It seemed to me that the bat was attracted by my passage on the road: it brushed by me, and abruptly out of the hovering darkness it swooped over my head and flew before me up the road. I felt comforted, exhilarated by the nearness of this buoyant and searching creature in the dusk. When I returned from the mailbox, the bat again seemed to accompany me, as if, in obedience to some obscure purpose in life, it too delighted in the companionship.

The warm weather held for another day or two, and then with that swiftness of deepening fall the days and nights turned cold. We did not see the bats again that year. Thinking on their sudden appearance and swift departure, we wondered where they had gone. Had they really flown south, far south, held aloft by that delicate membrane stretched between wrist and foot? How, I asked, could they pass the mountains in Canada, or survive the coastline and the stormy gulf? I imagined them making their way somehow, flitting from corridor to corridor, dependent on the insects still awake in that uncertain latitude.

Or had they found a crevice in a rock face nearby, some earth-warmed cavern unknown to us; and deep in that shelter drawn in upon themselves whatever their small bodies possessed, and gone to sleep for the winter? As the days shortened, I wondered what it would be like to be there with the bats, wherever they were in the darkness and frost, clinging in sleep to a precarious edge, waiting for spring—perhaps to freeze and never awake.

"Bats have few enemies. Bad weather is one of them. When not hibernating, they seem unable to endure long fasts; protracted cold, windy, rainy weather that keeps insects from flying, causes considerable mortality."[1]

For the rest of us plodding, terrestrial creatures snow came soon, and the year plunged deeper into frost.

The following year in late September I hiked down into Banner Creek from Campbell's hill on my way home from hunting. Halfway down the open hillside I stopped briefly to look inside a dilapidated frame shack left behind by miners a few years before. It was nearly dusk, and the light inside the shack was poor. But as my eyes became accustomed to the gloom, I found that I was not alone in the shack. My attention was caught by a dark, rounded shape on the wall near a window, halfway up from the floor. I stepped quietly over to it and found a small bat clinging to a crack in one of the boards. I had no light, and I could not see clearly any details of the creature, but it seemed to me that it was awake and that a pair of bright, steady eyes was watching me. I had a momentary impulse to pick it up and carry it outdoors where I could have a better look at it. I decided not to disturb it. I might have learned more, but I felt that it would not be worth the risk of scaring or injuring the bat.

I left the shack and quietly shut the door. The door had been closed when I came, and the bat had apparently entered through a hole in the eaves or by a broken window pane.

A week later a pair of bats again came to the yard on a mild evening and flew about as before until long after dark. When the warm evenings ended, they once more left us. They visited us in this way for three or four years—each fall when the south wind had blown the last leaves from the birches and the woods were silent and waiting. That rare warm evening would come, and the dusk took on life again.

I do not remember having seen them before and not often since. During that same period there were scattered reports of bats seen near Fairbanks in the evenings by people who did not know they existed so far north. It is likely that in milder years since that time these small bats have come and gone in other neighborhoods, and mostly unnoticed by people in lighted houses. Not long ago a neighbor mining on nearby Banner Creek reported to me that he had seen a bat while he was working outdoors in the evening.

It may be that from time to time a change in the climate of the interior, so slight that we did not otherwise notice it, extended their range northwards; or that a subtle shift in the pattern of their migration brought them to the river, to the yard and open field above it. And then, like so many other events in our lives, perhaps there is no explanation at all. A wind from a great, hidden tree blew in our direction one evening and, like leaves loosened from a shaken bough, they came and they vanished.

Despite the shadowy undertones of folk literature and old wives' tales—the imagery of fear and transformation, of witchcraft and brooms, my own recollections of the terror shown by my mother and grandmother at the very thought of having a bat in the house—I have never felt uneasiness in their presence. I remember an incident years ago when I was student in Washington. I came home late one night to the rooming house where I lived; as I climbed to the landing on the second floor, I saw a large bat flying up and down the corridor. It flew swiftly, avoiding me each time it passed. The mid-fall evening was warm, and the bat may have been attracted by the moths that were fluttering at the landing light. I was concerned that the bat would be trapped and injured, and before going upstairs to my room I opened a window at one end of the corridor.

"They are not witches... They will not try to get into your hair. Like most animals and some people, what they want is to be left alone."[2]

Though surely indifferent to our presence, as all wild things tend to be, they seemed to us in that far place, at the uttermost limit of their range, remote from the attics and belfries, from all folklore and superstition—remote from every human infringement that has so often determined the existence of their kind—to be warm, curious and friendly creatures whose lives momentarily touched our own. When they did not come again, we felt that something of a rare kinship was absent in the October twilight.

To think from this diminished prospective in time, from this long vista of empty light and deepening shadow, that so small and refined a creature could fill an uncertain niche in the world; and that its absence would leave, not just a momentary gap in nature, but a lack in one's own existence, one less possibility of being.

As if we were to look out on a cherished landscape, hoping to see on the distant, wrinkled plain, among the cloud-shadows passing over its face, groups of animals feeding and resting; and in the air above them a compact flock of waterfowl swiftly winging its way to a farther pond; and higher still, a watchful hawk on the wind. To look, straining one's eyesight, noting each detail of lake, meadow and bog; and to find nothing, nothing alive and moving. Only the wind and the distance, the silence of a vast, creatureless earth.

John Haines

1. Henry Hill Collins, Jr., *Complete Field Guide to North American Wildlife*, New York: Harper & Bros., 1958, p. 267.
2. Collins, *Ibid.*

A REQUIEM FOR THE ARCTIC REFUGE

No sign of life, no bird calls,
no mating cries from the tundra…

Only the strewn wreckage of a passing
illness—the discards of metal
and trash left behind by those
who write sorrow on the earth,
and leave to renew their plunder.

I remember, and so must you,
the lost sweetness of this land,
and far to the south a people
for whom it was home, driven to
forage your crime-cemented streets.

I hear a voice from another age
that would speak to us now:
"Forests precede civilization,
and deserts follow…"

Tell me, citizens in your lighted
houses:
        Is this what you wish
for our loaned and borrowed future?
When your houses are darkened
and your stations shut down,
your thousand-year dreampipe emptied…

And of our lost earth-bound refuge,

only a broad sheet of white paper
once held by an official hand—
now certified and fingerprinted,
smudged and stained with oil.

Michelangelo's "Night" *(Photo credit: George M. Grouras, Michelangelo-Night, The Sagrestria Nuova at the Medici Chapel.jpg; [1526-1531] Wikimedia Creative Commons)*

Background information:

1. The poem is spoken in the voice of a sibyl, or oracle, as represented here by Michelangelo's immense reclining female figure of *Night* in the Medici Chapel in Florence. Into the base of the sculpture are carved both a tragic mask and the figure of an owl. Asked once what his figure of *Night* might say if she could speak, Michelangelo replied that she would say, "Wake me not..." (From *The Owl and the Mask of the Dreamer*, p. 269).

2. Michelangelo himself replied, speaking in the person of Night: *Dear to me is sleep, and dearer to be of stone while wrongdoing and shame prevail; not to see, not to hear, is a great blessing: so do not awaken me; speak softly.* (From 100swallows at wordpress.com on January 31, 2009).

NIGHT

Do not wake me, for I am not ready
to speak, to break the spell
fixed in these sleeping stones.

Go quietly here. Whisper to wise men
what you cannot speak aloud.
Quiet the metal doors.

It is the time of earth-changes,
of vanishing rainfall,
and the restless barking of dogs.

Divided is the man of hidden
purpose, and evil his redemption.

Harness the wind and drive the water,
you that govern,
who yoke and stride the world…

And then be still.

Leaves of the one standing tree
fall through the twilight;
the night born images rise, the owl

in the mask of the dreamer wakes:
Who is the guest?
Who is it who knocks and whispers?

As one calmed in his death-dream
would never return
to this hunted world—

one more key to the clockwork
that drives the stunned machine,
another cry under the wheel...

But calmed and stationed aloft,
delight in his distance,
to see on the star-pavilions

the bright, imperial creatures rise,
ascend their thrones, rule
and prosper. The thrones darken,

earth in the moon-shadow fails,
and he alone in that cold
and drifting waste keeps alight

memorial constellations...

So I in this quiet sleep of stone
can say to you: Leave to me
this one sustaining solace—

my night that has more night
to come. To the sun that has set,
whose dawn I cannot see...

Mute in my transformation,
and do not wake me.

ARLINGTON

The pallor of so many
small white stones,
the metal in their names,
somber and strange
the calm of my country.

My father buried here,
and his father,
so many obedient lives.

And I too in my time
might have come,
but there is no peace
in this ground for me.

These fields of death
ask for broken columns,
a legend in pitted bronze
telling of the city
pulled into rubble here.

The soil should be thick
with shrapnel
and splinters of bone;

for a shrine, a lamp
fueled with blood,
if blood would burn.

Vincent van Gogh *(Photo credit: Vincent van Gogh—Portrait National Gallery of Art.jpg; [1853-1890] Wikimedia Creative Commons)*

ON A CERTAIN FIELD IN AUVERS

There is something in my heart...
 —Van Gogh

    I

On the road to Hallucination,
pass by the yellow house
that is the house of friendship,
but is also the color of madness...

Stand by the roadside, braced
in the punishing wind that blows
on that field and another...

In the red dust of evening,
ask yourself these questions:

'Who made the sun, strenuous
and burning?'
          It was I.

'And the cypress, a green torrent
in the nightwind?'
          It was I.

'And the clock of evening, coiled
like a spring?...Who turned
the stars in their sockets
and set them to spinning?'
                    It was I.

On the road to the Night Café,
where the light from a door
that is always open
spills over cobbles and tables;

where the pipesmoker calmed
his fury, a yellow chair
in which no one is sitting...

It is no one. It is I.

    II

I, who never for one hour
forgot how the light seizes
both field and striding sower;

who held my hand steady
in the solar flame, and drank
for my thirst the fiery
mineral spirit of the earth.

Who remembered always, even
in the blistering south,
a cellar in the north
where a handful of stunted
people peeled their substance
day by day, and all their
dumb and patient misery
steeped in a cold green light.

On the road to the hospital
built of the great stones
of sorrow, and furnished
with chains and pillows...
In the red dust of evening
the Angelus is ringing.

And out among the haystacks,
strange at this late hour,
a light, both moving and still,
as if someone there was
turning, a ring of candles
burning in his hatbrim...

It is...no one.

III

In the Asylum of Saint-Rémy,
that is also the burnt field
of Auvers; at the graveside
of two distracted brothers.

On this one day in July
we speak the rites for all
torn and departed souls.

And we hope that with
a hundred years of practice
we have learned to speak
the appropriate words:

'In the country of the deaf
a one-eared man was king…

'In the name of the poor,
and of the holy insane,
and the great light of the sun.'

John Meade Haines by Eric Deeter, Delta Community Library *(Permission courtesy of Gretchen Diemer; photo credit: Tiki Levinson)*

MEDITATION ON A SKULL CARVED IN CRYSTAL

To think that the world
lies wholly in this mind;
that this frozen water,
this clarity of quartz,
this ice, is all.

MAY THE OWL CALL AGAIN

At home in the glass house
of wit, keep watch
on the last conceit:

to say to oneself
in this fallen mirror
that the fog-drift of trees,
the inch of sky
in the well of windows—

these water-broken figures
entering and leaving
the last, drained pool
of light are all.

*

Within the artifact,
in the polished brilliance
of its mirror faces,
lies the bleached horror
of the empty skull
and its loosened hinges:

of the threadlike sutures parting,
and the drained blood
dried to this rusty scale.

Think of a house abandoned
to the cold chalks that score
the limits of dust:

the ear-ports catching wind,
the long porch of the nostrils
from which the watch-beetles
and the blue, predatory flies
have long since gnawed the solitude
and eaten the silence.

And where intelligence
kept its station,
arranging interior spaces,
opening windows toward
the shellshot lunar fields,
inhuman distances...

There is nothing to see
but a small green hollow
holding rain.

*

No one the color of darkness
sees entirely the shape of the sun.

But as the ocelot goes, smoldering,
spotted with fire, through the night—

Go now, return to water and mist.
You of the fireborn, go back to rain,

be what in the beginning you were:
seed of ice and brother to grain.

You with the glass mouth, drink
more silence. Be watchful, an eye

upturned in the soil of heaven.
And every shower rebuilds your face:

at the heart of your stillness,
the cry of a god trapped inside a star.

*

Blood into ice, and fur
into matted frost—
this is the way of winter,
on earth as in heaven.

Divided nostrils that smelt
of blood from afar;
the throat that drank it,
the lips and tongue
that thirsted:

changed into that which
is shone upon, that
which mirrors, and that
which sees if looked upon.

Nothing of beast or man
remains, of the stroked fur
and the aroused flesh;
but the filed teeth fixed
in their glitter,
a smile of ferocious peace.

*

Burn sacrifice, for all
that was clear has darkened
in the burning glass.

Break open the breast-cage,
let the creature-heart redden
in the light that remains.

Swear by the fallen blood
and burnt savor of the flesh
that the sun will rise,
that the wheel of the calendar,
carved with its lunar faces,
will never stop turning.

Put death aside,
there is nothing to fear
from the sleep-walking spirits
in this darkness
not wholly of the night.

The great stone hall is quiet:
these pillars and dreaming cases,
a household
calmed at nightfall.

Now, as the smoke of sacrifice
disperses through chilled
and vacant rooms,
the white ash deadens and falls.

Sleep, for the changed heartbeat
knocks and is still...

In place of the lamp
that was lighted,
a drop of blood inside the sun.

    *

As if the pain of thought,
by repeated blows, would be
nothing but light in the end.

Stare into this well of shadows,
drained and never empty:
all nomenclatures, measurements
by meter and inch forgotten.

Beyond the dark slates of water
and sunlight, how the stone
jaw slides on its hinges,
how the nostrils quicken,
and the glassy brow crowns
the eyes, sunken and gleaming.

All suns, all moons, all days
find their completion here,
as blood finds its pool of quiet
where the mercury sleeps, and night
with its pallor of threads
draws the sutures closer.

The cold hours pass;
a fire-seed fumes, blown
once more into life.
The star-crossed lattice
brightens; day begins,
as empty, as filled
with floating shadows,
voices waking as before.

*

Of the dissolution
of fabrics and structures,
the breaking
of cemented boundaries:

Improvisations—names
that vanish among
the catalogues that vanish,
all their complexities
strung with spittle:

Hierarchies, lists of the
flowering and cheeping world:
of these, and what
we knew this life to be,

death is the last confusion.

After the smoky anguish
of your dying
comes this resolution:

the opening calm, a blue
thoughtbound space
in which there are signal
lights, globed fires
giving way to night.

*

Intelligence is what we find,
gazing into rock as into water
at the same depth shining.

Mirror, glazed forehead of snow.
Holes for its eyes, to see
what the dead see dying:

a grain of ice in the stellar
blackness, lighted
by a sun, distant within.

PART III.

Appendix

CORRESPONDENCE TIMELINE

2009

March 15 – Email
March 16
April 1 – I met John for the first time. He was guest speaker for the Alaska Writer Laureates' event, UAA Campus Bookstore.
April 8 – with card
April 24 – with *Weimar, Germany: Promise and Tragedy*, the cover and chapter 1, by Eric Weitz
May 3 – with "Tales of Resistance" *Time Magazine,* V-Day Special Issue
May 14 – with card
June 8
June 13
June 16 – Email
June 24 – "The Horny Shepherd To His Love" (1953)
June 24 – Email
June 26 – Two emails
June 28 – I met John again when he came to Anchorage for the USA Artists gathering and to celebrate his birthday.
July 8 – with "The UA Dunciad," by Bernard Meade (1998, Montana)
July 18
July 27
August 6 – with the essay "On The Street" (2006)
August 18
August 21
August 22
August 23
August 27 – with "The Elder Birch" (2007) and "To The Century's End" (1999)
September 2 – postcard
September 7
September 13

October 2 – with card
October 29
November 15
November 28
December 11
December 21

2010

January (no date) – with card and photo
January 7
January 17
February 5
February 19
March 1 – John Haines spoke at the "Rosa Luxemburg Remembered" event, UAA Campus Bookstore
March 5 – with two "Letters to the Editor"
March 18
April 2
April 9 – with *Guardian Weekly* article, "Laptops no longer welcome" by Daniel de Vise
April 18 – postcard
April 28
May 6 – with email from Bruce Guernsey
May 17
May 24 – with card
June 1 – with Kliban painting
June 6
June 13
June 24
July 9 – with card
July 21
August 14
August 27

September 17 – with limerick (2009)
October 6 – with card
October 23
November 8 – with card
November 22
November 25 – with card
December 17 – with "Epitaph For A Young Man" (1953)

2011

January 10
January 23 – with card

NOTES

A Note about John's Father John Meade Haines, 1894-1969

John Haines graduated from the U.S. Naval Academy at Annapolis, Class of 1918. He retired as a U.S. Navy Rear Admiral.

Awards and Citations: Navy Cross
Awarded for actions during the World War II.

The President of the United States of America takes pleasure in presenting the Navy Cross to Commander John Meade Haines, United States Navy, for extraordinary heroism and distinguished service in the line of his profession as Force Commander. Submarine Squadron SIXTEEN, for aggressive and successful conduct of a Marine-Submarine Raider Expedition from 8 August 1942. As Force Commander of naval units, Commander Haines' displayed great skill and courage in carrying out an untried and hazardous mission. Although harassed by enemy aircraft and maneuvering his vessels in immediate proximity to an enemy-controlled coast, he succeeded in effecting an undetected landing of Marines against an alert enemy and later effected a highly successful withdrawal. He also directed the ships in his command to fire on two enemy ships in the lagoon, which were sunk by gunfire. His courage and skill in the handling of the vessels of his command on this occasion were in keeping with the highest traditions of the naval service.

Action Date: August 17 & 18, 1942
Service: Navy
Rank: Commander
Division: Submarine Squadron 18

(From The Hall of Valor Project: https://valor.militarytimes.com/)
(For fascinating insights into John Meade Haines' upbringing and lineage see his brother's obituary, "Robert "Baines" Haines (1926-2019)," by Joe Ditter, The Coronado Times, 02/05/2019 (https://coronadotimes.com/news/2019/02/05/robert-baines-haines-1926-2019)

A Note about Jorge Manrique, 1440-1479

Jorge Manrique was the son of Rodrigo, Grand Master of Santiago and was born at Paredes de Nava. From his birth, he was in the midst of wars, and he joined his father in supporting Alfonso and Isabel of Castile in their claims for the throne. He was killed before the walls of Garcia-Munoz in his thirty-ninth year.

"Coplas por la muerte de su padre" ("Stanzas about the Death of his Father") was composed upon the death of Manrique's valiant father, Don Rodrigo, in 1476, and achieved immortality in Spanish literature. The entire poem consists of 40 stanzas that examine three lives: The terrestrial life that ends in death; the life of fame that lasts longer; and the eternal life, or life after death, that has no end.

(From Jorge Manrique—Wikipedia, with references from *Love and Remembrance: The Poetry of Jorge Manrique* by Frank A. Dominguez.)

A Note about Rosa Luxemburg

The event, Rosa Luxemburg Remembered, was held at the UAA Campus Bookstore on March 1, 2010.

Poet John Meade Haines, History Professors Elizabeth Dennison, William Myers and Andrew Janco discussed the extraordinary political and social activist, theoretician and revolutionary Rosa Luxemburg, 1871-1919. Her life in Germany, prison letters, as well as theories regarding revolution, spontaneity and class were addressed.

According to Professor Elizabeth Dennison, Rosa participated fully in the German revolutionary movement and was repeatedly arrested for inciting violence and for inciting public disobedience, particularly in regard to criticizing the German government and its militarism. In June 1914, Rosa was arrested for her public accusation that the army maltreated soldiers; 1,013 soldiers volunteered to testify in her defense and the trial was suspended.

Rosa was deeply depressed over the outbreak of WW I and served a total of 3 years and 4 months in prison. Her collection of letters addressed to Sophie Liebknecht from this time period are filled with small details of the prison world—birds and their songs, trees and berries, sunsets, and poetry. Her transfer to a different prison was marked by the unhappiness of leaving the birds and prison garden. The war years brought great personal hardship and loss to her, including the death of loved ones at the front.

IN MEMORY OF ROSA LUXEMBURG, 1871-1919
By John Meade Haines
(Poem recited on March 1, 2010)

Dear Rosa, I want to say: Come back, we need you now.
We know you are gone, have been for over a century,
yet, you are here, have been, and will be
for those of us who read, who listen and remember.
We need your thought, your love, your
unfailing memory of events and losses,
with no remembered love forsaken.

As you have spoken in a letter to a friend:
"Oh, this 'sublime silence of eternity'
in which so many screams have faded away unheard.
It rings within me so strongly that I have
no special corner of my heart reserved for ghosts.
I am at home wherever in the world there are
clouds, birds, and human tears."

PUBLICATIONS AND SELECTED RECORDINGS

Books and Chap Books

Winter News (1966)

El amor ascendia, by Miguel Hernandez, translation (1967)

Suite for the Pied Piper (1968)

The Legend of Paper Plates (1970)

The Stone Harp (1971)

The Mirror (1971)

Twenty Poems (1971)

Leaves and Ashes (1974)

The Sun on Your Shoulder (1976)

In Five Years Time (1976) essay

Cicada (1977)

In A Dusty Light (1977)

Of Traps and Snares (1981) essays

Living Off the Country: Essays on Poetry and Place (1981)

Other Days (1982) essays

News From the Glacier: Selected Poems, 1960-1980 (1982)

In the Forest Without Leaves (1984)

Stories We Listened To (1986) essays

Meditation on a Skull Carved in Crystal (1989)

The Stars, the Snow, the Fire: Twenty-Five Years in the Alaska Wilderness (1989) essays

Rain Country (1990)

New Poems: 1980-88 (1990)

The Owl in the Mask of the Dreamer: Collected Poems (1993; 1996)

Where the Twilight Never Ends (1994)

Fables and Distances, New and Selected Essays (1996)

A Guide to the Four-Chambered Heart (1996)

At the End of This Summer, Poems 1948-1954 (1997)

For The Century's End, Poems 1990-1999 (2001)

Of Your Passage, O Summer: Uncollected Poems from the 1960's (2004)

Descent: Selected Essays, Reviews, and Letters (2010)

Selected Recordings

April 10, 1967, Poetry Center Digital Archive San Francisco State University.

(61:10) https://diva.sfsu.edu/collections/poetrycenter/bundles/222896

June 1984, "Crossing the Boundaries," Sitka Summer Writers' Symposium, The Island Institute, Sitka, Alaska. John Haines reads "Forest without leaves" with music composed by John Clement Adams (aka John Luther Adams). 1 audiocassette (60:00). UAF Rasmuson, Oral History 2017-16-01, Level 2.

May 13, 1992, Elliston Poetry Reading University of Cincinnati. 18 tracks. https://drc.libraries.uc.edu

June 1993, "Sitka Symposium on Human Values and the Written Word, A Tenth Anniversary Celebration," The Island Institute, Sitka, Alaska. 2 audiocassette tapes: Faculty Readings: John Haines & Hugh Brody, and Faculty Lecture by John Haines.

December 8, 2005, Library of Congress Archive of Recorded Poetry and Literature, John Haines reading his poems. 2 sound discs (1 hr., 24 min.), ICD 24142-24143 (playback copy).

2008, *Winter Light, the poetry of John Haines* CD, 77 poems and 4 essays read by the author. https://open.spotify.com/album/36kMS4rKjsORh6DsPgig7c

April 1, 2009, Alaska Writer Laureates' Panel, Parts 1 & 2, University of Alaska Anchorage Campus Bookstore. Recording available through Archives and Special Collections at the UAA/APU Consortium Library. Collection number UAA-0152. Guide to the Bookstore special events records 1999-2019. https://archives.consortiumlibrary.org/?s=uaa+bookstore

INDEX OF WRITINGS

Poems and essays in *May the Owl Call Again: A Return to Poet John Meade Haines, 1924-2011*.

2   "In the Forest Without Leaves" XI

16 "Winter News"

17 Two after Li Po: "Conversation"

17 Two after Li Po: "Quiet Night"

18 "Untitled"

19 "With An Axe and An Auger," essay

24 "Into the Glacier"

25 "Poem"

27 "In the Forest Without Leaves" XII

43 "The Horny Shepherd to His Love"

47 "The UA Dunciad, Some Mock-Heroics on a Renewable Theme"

54 "On the Street," essay

68 "The Elder Birch"

69 "To the Century's End"

92 Letters to The Editor, *Fairbanks Daily News-Miner,* August 30, 2002

94 Letters to The Editor, *The Atlantic Monthly,* September 10, 2004

122 "Limerick"

134 "Epitaph for a Young Man"

144 "If the Owl Calls Again"

150 "Rain Country"

156 "In the Forest Without Leaves" XV

158 "The Ice Child"

160 "Fourth of July at Santa Ynez"

162	"The Snowbound City"
163	"The Creative Spirit in Art and Literature," essay
170	"Wartime: A Late Memoir," essay
172	"The Glutton"
175	"Missoula in a Dusty Light"
177	"To Vera Thompson"
183	"Poem of the Forgotten"
184	"Tenderfoot"
185	"Fairbanks Under the Solstice"
186	"Harvest"
187	"Little Cosmic Dust Poem"
188	"Return to Richardson, Spring 1981"
190	"Shadows II," essay
197	"A Requiem for the Arctic Refuge"
200	"Night"
202	"Arlington"
203	"On a Certain Field in Auvers"
207	"Meditation on a Skull Carved in Crystal"
222	"In Memory of Rosa Luxemburg"

PUBLISHER ACKNOWLEDGMENTS

Acknowledgement is made to the following publishers for the poems and essays that were previously published in *May the Owl Call Again: A Return to Poet John Meade Haines, 1924-2011*.

Winter News, Wesleyan University Press. 1966. "Fairbanks Under the Solstice," "If the Owl Calls Again," "Into the Glacier," "Poem," "Poem of the Forgotten," "Winter News."

The Stone Harp, Wesleyan University Press. 1971. "The Snowbound City," "To Vera Thompson."

Cicada, Wesleyan University Press. 1977. "Arlington," "Fourth of July at Santa Ynez."

In A Dusty Light, Graywolf Press. 1977. "Harvest," "Missoula in a Dusty Light."

The poems mentioned above (excluding "The Snowbound City" and "Fourth of July at Santa Ynez") from *Winter News*, *The Stone Harp*, *Cicada*, and *In A Dusty Light* were also included in the collection *News from the Glacier, Selected Poems 1960-1980*, Wesleyan University Press. 1982.

We Make A Fire: Orca Anthology of Poems and Prose, edited by Cheryl Morse, Orca Press. 1982. "Shadows II."

Zyzzyva, Vol. III, No. 3, Fall 1987. "Meditation on a Skull Carved in Crystal" (Highlighted in the book is this version of the poem). Also published by Brooding Heron Press, Waldron Island, 1989.

The Stars, the Snow, The Fire: Twenty-Five Years in the Alaska Wilderness, Graywolf Press. 1989, 2000. "With An Axe and An Auger."

New Poems: 1980-88, Story Line Press. 1990, 1992. "In the Forest Without Leaves," "Little Cosmic Dust Poem," "Meditation on a Skull Carved in Crystal," "On a Certain Field in Auvers," "Rain Country," "Tenderfoot."

Note: All of the poems mentioned above were published in the collection *The Owl in the Mask of the Dreamer*, Graywolf Press, 1993. In the 1996 edition, the poems "The Glutton" and "Night" were added.

Fables and Distances: New and Selected Essays, Graywolf Press. 1996. "The Creative Spirit in Art and Literature."

For the Century's End, Poems 1990-1999, University of Washington Press. 2001. "The Ice Child."

Of Your Passage, O Summer; Uncollected Poems from the 1960s, Limberlost Press. 2004. Two after Li Po: "Conversation," Two after Li Po: "Quiet Night," "Untitled," "Return to Richardson, Spring 1981."

Alaska Reader: Voices from the North, edited by Anne Hanley and Carolyn Kremers, Chicago Review Press-Fulcrum. 2005. "A Requiem for the Arctic Refuge." The poem was also published in *Ice-Floe* 5, no. 1, Summer Solstice 2004; *onEarth*, Winter 2005.

Descent: Selected Essays, Reviews, and Letters, CavanKerry Press. 2010. "On the Street," "Wartime: A Late Memoir."

Note: *Permafrost Magazine*, founded in 1977 in Fairbanks, Alaska, with editorial assistance from author Jean Anderson, published earlier versions of many of John Haines' poems and essays. Vol. 2, No. 1, Fall 1978 featured "On a Skull Carved in Crystal" and Vol. 3, No. 1, Fall 1979 featured "Rain Country." Photos of the Richardson homestead and one of John Haines with his friend/mentor Fred Campbell were included in the 1979 issue. These issues can be found at: https://scholarworks.alaska.edu/bitstream/handle/11122/1646/Permafrost%20V2%20No%201.pdf?sequence=1&isAllowed=y and https://scholarworks.alaska.edu/bitstream/handle/11122/1620/Permafrost%20V3%20No%201.pdf?sequence=1&isAllowed=y

ABOUT THE AUTHOR

(Photo credit: Cynthia Lee Steele)

Rachel Epstein was the Special Events Coordinator at the University of Alaska Anchorage Campus Bookstore from 1999-2020. She is the proud recipient of the 2012 Contributions to Literacy in Alaska Award (CLIA), the 2020 Alaska Governor's Award for Distinguished Service to the Humanities in Education, and the 2023 University of Alaska Anchorage Meritorious Award.

ABOUT CIRQUE PRESS

Cirque Press grew out of *Cirque*, a literary journal that publishes the works of writers and artists from the North Pacific Rim, a region that reaches north from Oregon to the Yukon Territory, south through Alaska to Hawaii, and west to the Russian Far East.

Cirque Press is a partnership of Sandra Kleven, publisher, and Michael Burwell, editor. Ten years ago, we recognized that works of talented writers in the region were going unpublished, and the Press was launched to bring those works to fruition. We publish fiction, nonfiction, and poetry, and we seek to produce art that provides a deeper understanding about the region and its cultures. The writing of our authors is significant, personal, and strong.

Sandra Kleven – Michael Burwell, publishers and editors
www.cirquejournal.com

BOOKS FROM CIRQUE PRESS

Apportioning the Light by Karen Tschannen (2018)

The Lure of Impermanence by Carey Taylor (2018)

Echolocation by Kristin Berger (2018)

Like Painted Kites & Collected Works by Clifton Bates (2019)

Athabaskan Fractal: Poems of the Far North by Karla Linn Merrifield (2019)

Holy Ghost Town by Tim Sherry (2019)

Drunk on Love: Twelve Stories to Savor Responsibly by Kerry Dean Feldman (2019)

Wide Open Eyes: Surfacing from Vietnam by Paul Kirk Haeder (2020)

Silty Water People by Vivian Faith Prescott (2020)

Life Revised by Leah Stenson (2020)

Oasis Earth: Planet in Peril by Rick Steiner (2020)

The Way to Gaamaak Cove by Doug Pope (2020)

Loggers Don't Make Love by Dave Rowan (2020)

The Dream That Is Childhood by Sandra Wassilie (2020)

Seward Soundboard by Sean Ulman (2020)

The Fox Boy by Gretchen Brinck (2021)

Lily Is Leaving: Poems by Leslie Ann Fried (2021)

One Headlight by Matt Caprioli (2021)

November Reconsidered by Marc Janssen (2021)

Callie Comes of Age by Dale Champlin (2021)

Someday I'll Miss This Place Too by Dan Branch (2021)

Out There In The Out There by Jerry McDonnell (2021)

Fish the Dead Water Hard by Eric Heyne (2021)

Salt & Roses by Buffy McKay (2022)

Growing Older In This Place: A Life in Alaska's Rainforest by Margo Wasserman Waring (2022)

Kettle Dance: A Big Sky Murder by Kerry Dean Feldman (2022)

Nothing Got Broke by Larry F. Slonaker (2022)

On the Beach: Poems 2016-2021 by Alan Weltzien (2022)

Sky Changes on the Kuskokwim by Clifton Bates (2022)

Transplanted By Birgit Lennertz Sarrimanolis (2022)

Between Promise and Sadness by Joanne Townsend (2022)

Yosemite Dawning by Shauna Potocky (2022)

The Woman Within by Tami Phelps and Kerry Dean Feldman (2023)

In the Winter of the Orange Snow by Diane S. Carpenter (2023)

Mail Order Nurse by Sue Lium (2023)

All in Due Time by Kate Troll (2023)

Infinite Meditations For Inspiration and Daily Practice by Scott Hanson (2023)

Getting Home from Here by Anne Ward-Masterson (2023)

Crossing the Burnside Bridge & Other Poems by Janice D. Rubin (2023)

A Variable Sense of Things by Ron McFarland (2023)

May the Owl Call Again: A Return to Poet John Meade Haines, 1924-2011 by Rachel Epstein (2024)

PRAISE FOR *MAY THE OWL CALL AGAIN: A RETURN TO POET JOHN MEADE HAINES, 1924-2011*

What a fine tribute this collection is. That Rachel Epstein corresponded so frequently with John in his last years is both touching and laudable. He clearly appreciated the long-distance friendship. I was saddened by the elder poet's references to loneliness and failing health while simultaneously uplifted by his endlessly inquisitive mind, sense of humor, and ongoing interest in literature and the arts. Re-reading the poems and essays included here, I was moved again by the wistful and sometimes dark tone and the seeming simplicity of language. John Haines will be remembered as one of Alaska's greatest thinkers and writers.

—Anne Coray, poet and author of *Bone Strings*

Alaskan poet John Haines has been gone for more than a decade now, but his singular voice stays with me—the deep quiet of it and its enchantment, the spareness of his lines—Li Po transposed to the far north. Much else is here to muse on and admire—his charming letters to Rachel Epstein, photos of his homestead in Richardson, transcripts of talks given, memoirs of a vanished Alaska, selected essays, notes on the imagination's relationship with the natural world, even recollections of his service on a destroyer in the Pacific toward the end of WW II. *May the Owl Call Again* is a moving and memorable collection, and at its heart is Haines' haunting poetry.

—Marc Hudson, poet, translator, and an emeritus professor at Wabash College. His most recent book of poems is *East Of Sorrow*.

May the Owl Call Again bears witness to the last years of Haines' life—his thoughts, humor, melancholy, a profound awareness of Alaska's rhythms, and his struggles with engagement in a broken world. But, above all, it is a meditation on friendship and the solace of intimacy that can be found in the handwritten page. It's a testament to care, the aches of connection and solitude, and the consolation of finding kinship with another. I found myself reading it all at once and walking away with a profound sense of gratitude for Epstein sharing this Haines with all of us.

—Freya Rohn, poet and founder of Ariadne Archive

Rachel Epstein artfully constructs a sensitive portrait of poet, John Haines, in the evenfall of his life, through a series of letters exchanged with the author. Revealed in this correspondence is a man with a giant intellect, a deep curiosity, and a true interest in the present-day world. His reputation as curmudgeon is not evident as he writes to Epstein about cats, sends her cards (mostly cats, mostly humorous), and comments on life while exhibiting a dry wit and wry sense of humor. He recommends films and books related to interests she has expressed. In this, he proves himself to be a generous and attentive friend. In addition to the letters, Epstein includes a broad selection of poetry that reflects the range and content of Haines' work. I was particularly glad to see she included "Rain Country," a poem I have reread over the decades. I still find myself drawn into that country anew, as if reading the poem for the first time, the poet *not old, not yet*. Ultimately, Epstein's purpose in writing this book is best expressed by her: *My hope is that John Haines will not fade from collective memory but will continue to influence, inspire, and nurture creative expression within and beyond Alaska.* Her fine work represents a great contribution to that effort.

—Gretchen Diemer, poet and author of *Between Fire and Water, Ice and Sky*

www.ingramcontent.com/pod-product-compliance
Lightning Source LLC
LaVergne TN
LVHW020435070526
838199LV00032B/632/J